World Food
SPAIN

MARKS &
SPENCER

BEVERLY LEBLANC

World Food
SPAIN

Marks and Spencer p.l.c.
Baker Street, London, W1U 8EP
www.marksandspencer.com

Created and produced by The Bridgewater Book Company Ltd.
Project Editor Stephanie Horner
Project Designer Michael Whitehead
Photography David Jordan
Home Economist Judy Williams
Additional photography Max Alexander and Alistair Plumb

ISBN: 1-84273-930-1
Printed in China

NOTES FOR THE READER

- This book uses both metric and imperial measurements. Follow the same
  units of measurement throughout; do not mix metric and imperial.

- All spoon measurements are level: teaspoons are assumed to be 5 ml, and
  tablespoons are assumed to be 15 ml.

- Unless otherwise stated, milk is assumed to be full fat, eggs and individual
  vegetables such as potatoes are medium, and pepper is freshly ground
  black pepper.

- Recipes using raw or very lightly cooked eggs should be avoided by infants,
  the elderly, pregnant women, convalescents, and anyone suffering from
  an illness.

- The times given are an approximate guide only. Preparation times differ
  according to the techniques used by different people and the cooking times
  may also vary from those given.

contents

INTRODUCTION

Spanish cuisine is varied and rich, reflecting and preserving generations of regional traditions.

Anyone who has visited Spain's sprawling coastal Mediterranean resorts and returned home with the impression that Spaniards only cook paella and chicken in garlic to tourist standard, will have missed out on the vast diversity of dishes eaten every day. Although at first sight home cooking might appear simple and unadorned, meals are centred around quality ingredients, with an appreciation of seasonal freshness. Hospitality and generosity also influence the Spanish appreciation of well-prepared food.

Spain's position on the Iberian Peninsula also gives it an Atlantic coastline. This simple geographical fact, along with the massive size of the country, makes it difficult to summarize Spanish cooking. The centre of the country is a vast plateau with arid plains, fringed by landscapes that include Mediterranean and Atlantic coastlines and soaring mountain ranges, and the entire country can experience ferocious weather conditions ranging from searingly hot to fiercely cold. What someone from sunny Seville considers to be a 'typical' meal is unlikely to be described as 'typical' by a native of Pamplona.

Most Spanish food is robust and flavoursome, but the north–south culinary divide is easily recognizable: northern cooking tends to be richer than that of the south and features more meat and dairy products.

Culinary legacies

Contemporary Spanish cooks have much to thank ancient invaders for. The Phoenicians, who arrived about 1100 BC, established a trading settlement in

The warmth and vibrancy of Spain is reflected in its domestic architecture, as well as in its food

what has become Cadiz, planting the first grapevines in nearby Jerez. This southwest corner of Andalusia remains Spain's sherry-producing centre. Next came the Carthaginians, who made no significant culinary contributions. They were followed by the Romans, who planted the first olive trees, and thus produced the first of the now-essential oil, in about AD 210. When, in 711, the Arabian Moors conquered virtually the entire peninsula, except for Asturias and the Basque country, they expanded the groves. (Arab rule continued to 1492, when monarchs Ferdinand V and Isabella I became rulers of all Spain.)

The Moors designed and developed extensive irrigation systems, *huertas*, to support the crops they introduced to the peninsula. Both the vast irrigated farms and major cash crops survive to this day. Spanish tastes were changed forever with the successful cultivation of rice, citrus fruit, almonds and dates, and the introduction of spices from the Middle East. Aubergines, apricots, peaches and quinces were other Moorish imports, as well as coffee – the drink of choice for most Spanish adults today.

Homage is also paid to the Golden Age of Spanish exploration in just about every kitchen every day. There was a silver lining to Christopher Columbus' unsuccessful quest for a route to the East Indies to break the Venetian monopoly on the trade of the fabulously expensive spices – the discovery of the Caribbean islands in 1492. On his return to Spain he brought with him the bounty from the New World that was to change cooking not only in Spain, but also the whole Mediterranean. The hot and sweet peppers he introduced were instantly included in cooking, their use first spreading by word of mouth through the extensive network of monasteries.

Columbus also introduced tobacco, exotic new fruit and vegetables such as yams and sweet potatoes. On his third voyage in 1502, he captured a Mayan trading boat laden with the cocoa beans that were used as a trading currency. Ferdinand was unimpressed by the new commodity, and not until after 1528, when Hernán Cortés returned to Spain with the Aztec chocolate-making equipment, did chocolate become the rage at court and eventually all over Spain. The first commercial shipment of cocoa beans arrived in 1585; the trade has never ceased. The love affair continues, with *chocolaterías* in all towns and cities today. Columbus didn't live long enough to see his discovery become a hot drink, but for many Spaniards the traditional breakfast consists of deep-fried strips of choux pastry called *churros*, served with a glass of hot chocolate almost too thick to drink.

Although dishes with traditional Moorish influences abound, especially in restaurants, and cosmopolitan Spaniards still eat many dishes their grandparents enjoyed, Spanish cooking isn't preserved in aspic. Today, food processors and blenders are more likely

Barcelona's La Boqueria market ... has been trading since the 18th century

have been, with vendors selling shimmering seafood of all kinds, freshly butchered meat carcasses, preserved meat products and the most luscious-looking fruit and vegetables. Even in major cities, where more and more women work out of the home, market shopping flourishes. Barcelona's La Boqueria market, on Las Ramblas, the social heart of the city, for example, has been trading since the 18th century, and is one of the greatest in Europe. It is open throughout the day, but trade really picks up early evening as locals shop on their way home. (The small, café-style restaurants in the market cook meat and seafood to order, providing an inexpensive lunch stop – and the food could not be fresher.) And, bustling and vibrant as La Boqueria is, it is only one of several markets in the city, all thriving. Fusion cooking, the pairing of cuisines from different sides of the globe that is evident in other European countries, has had little influence here. Chinese restaurants do thrive in some large cities, but their flavourings, cooking techniques and ingredients are not incorporated in mainstream Spanish cooking.

Eating the Spanish way

It has been said that Spaniards eat all day and part of the night. Most urban workers start with a light breakfast and continue to eat and snack all day until they finally sit down to an evening meal, which can be as late as 10 pm. (For schoolchildren, the evening meal is *merienda*, served about 6 pm.)

The Spanish work day begins with *el desayuno*, a quick, light breakfast of coffee with a pastry, either at home or in a café or bar on the way to work. Coffee shops always offer a supply of fresh croissants and bread rolls, and in Madrid *churros con chocolate* are

Above *Storks return to their nests each year, flying in, like tourists, from foreign climes*

Overleaf *Painted houses form a colourful backdrop on the bank of the river in Girona, in Catalonia*

to be used than mortars and pestles, and modern kitchens feature all the latest appliances.

Spanish supermarkets are large and busy, and, of course, fast-food restaurants are springing up, but the tradition of daily market shopping for fresh fruit, vegetables and seafood continues. Market days in rural communities are as important as they always

Tapas bars open at about 1 pm, offering their array of delicacies, which are enjoyed before la comida, *the main meal of the day*

a traditional treat that were once sold from vendors on every street corner. Today, these long, thin deep-fried fritters, dusted with sugar and cinnamon, are served with a cup of rich, dark Spanish hot chocolate at *churrerías* and cafés. For office workers, by 10 or 10.30 am it is time for an espresso and perhaps a slice of cake or a pastry, just to take the edge off their hunger. Or they might stop around 11 am for *las onces* (elevenses), or for *almuerzo* (lunch), depending on when they prefer their main meal. Tapas bars open at about 1 pm, offering their array of delicacies (see page 35), which are enjoyed before *la comida*, the

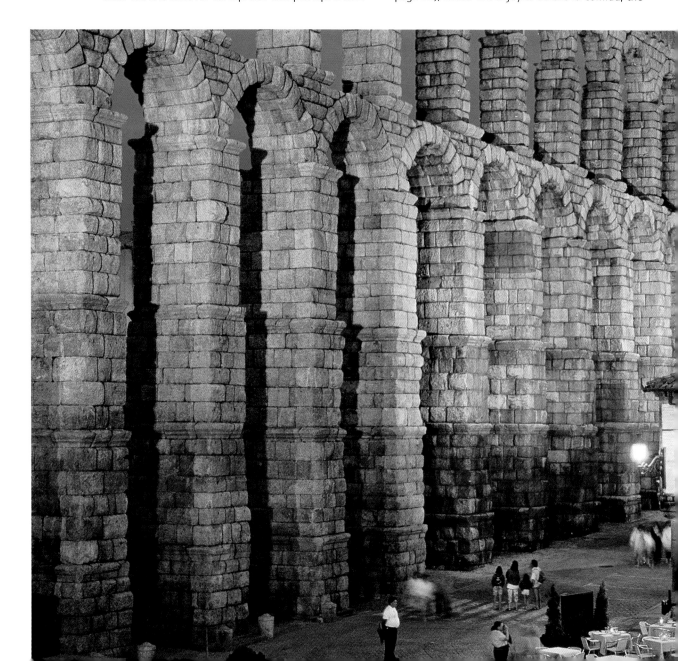

main meal of the day for many people. Offices generally close at 1.30 or 2 pm for several hours to allow employees to return home, where two or three small courses and a bottle of wine will be waiting. *La comida* for a working professional, for example, may consist of pasta or rice followed by sausages or steak or a fish dish, then fruit or yogurt. Sausages with Lentils (see page 147) is a typical *comida* dish, as are simplified versions of *cocidos*, which are Spanish hotpots (see page 32). Then it's back to work for a couple of hours. Afterwards many Spaniards will stop for a drink and tapas with colleagues on the way home. *La cena*, the evening meal, at home might be lighter than *la comida*, consisting of soup or omelette, followed by cheese or fruit. It will be eaten at about 8.30 pm in winter and more like 9.30 pm in summer. If dinner is at a restaurant, the booking will be about 10 pm for a leisurely three-course meal, finishing around midnight. After a good night's sleep it will be time for the following day's *desayuno*.

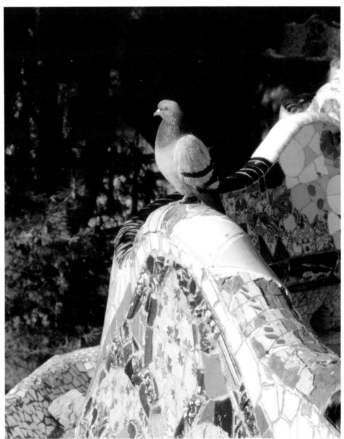

Above *The sinuous curves of Gaudi's work in the Park Guel in Barcelona*

Left *Imposing arches on a grand scale make a dramatic setting for dining alfresco*

Andalusia is home to many of the dishes foreigners think of as quintessentially Spanish

The Spanish regions

For the traveller through Spain, the cuisine varies with the scenery. Each region offers local specialities, treating similar ingredients differently to produce distinctive flavours. Tortilla, the humble thick, flat egg-and-potato omelette, is one of the few dishes usually available everywhere, but even that is prepared with regional variations (see page 42). Not surprisingly, the natural partners for regional dishes are the local wines.

Andalusia

This is the land of flamenco dancing, bullfights and beautiful, elegant Moorish architecture. A traditional dish in Córdoba, in the heart of ancient Arab Spain, is *rabo de toro*, or bulltail stew. Elsewhere, the region's cuisine showcases the Moorish legacy in Spanish cooking with the abundant use of spices and dried and fresh fruit. Andalusia is home to many of the dishes foreigners think of as quintessentially Spanish. Chilled tomato-and-pepper Gazpacho (see page 99), for example, is one of the best-known soups in the world, and a pitcher of chilled Sangria (see page 253), the red wine and fruit punch, immediately evokes images of sunny Spain. The azure-blue Mediterranean waters supply constant seafood, and the semi-arid land supports fruit-laden vineyards and olive groves. The picturesque *bodegas* of Jerez produce the finest sherries in the world.

The heat and long hours of sunshine mean there is an abundance of large sweet peppers, juicy tomatoes, oil-rich olives and citrus fruit, as well as a dazzling array of fruit that northern Europeans consider exotic, but which are commonplace here – figs, pomegranates, persimmons and passion fruit. A dish described as *a la andaluza* will contain a colourful, thirst-quenching mixture of peppers, tomatoes and possibly fruit. Seville oranges, so favoured by the British to make marmalade, are only grown around Seville, and the use of their bitter juice appears in recipes from the Middle Ages.

The variety of tapas served in Seville's restaurants and bars is renowned. The deep-fried dishes, such as Deep-fried Seafood (see page 159), are especially good – no one who drives along the Costa del Sol coast road will be disappointed at even the most humble seaside restaurant with a plate of fried squid rings (*calamares*). It's not for nothing that Andalusia is known as the 'frying pan of Spain', or the *zona de los fritos* – the region of fried foods.

Inland, the terrain is more rugged, with breath-taking mountain roads that eventually reach Spain's highest peaks, the snow-capped Sierra Nevada. Here, in villages such as Jabugo and Trevélez, you find the cured air-dried mountain ham, *jamón serrano* (see page 32), prized the world over for its tender, salty meat. It can flavour cooked dishes, such as Paprika Chicken on a Bed of Onions and Ham (see page 131), but to appreciate its character, nibble unadorned slices while sipping *fino* sherry before a meal.

Aragon

Medieval hill-top towns with rough stone houses dot this ancient kingdom that nestles along the Pyrenees. Here, Arab and Christian cultures thrived together. The region is landlocked, with a varying and harsh climate — summers can be scorching, while winter will be freezing, with heavy snowfalls.

Every coastal village has its fishing harbour. Tiny boats bring in the daily catch for the markets and restaurants

The fertile central basin along the Ebro River, near Zaragoza, yields vegetables, fruit and almonds, and ... flavoursome oil

Such extremes mean simple, hearty fare is the order of the day, although the Arab influence is evident in the spiced fruit desserts.

For hundreds of years, shepherds have tended the long-haired Lacha sheep that graze in the foothills and provide delicious meat and cheeses. The tradition of nomadic herders means Aragon has a culinary history of preserved foods, including air-dried hams and dried salt cod, that are easily transported without spoiling. This region also enjoys other good pork products, such as black pudding (*morcilla*), used to flavour a traditional lamb and white bean stew. Or the blood sausage is cooked in the dry cider drunk here, in dishes similar to those from Normandy in northern France. Numerous rivers give rise to many recipes in which trout features.

Robust *chilindrón* stews, made with lamb, chicken or pork, such as Pork with Peppers (see page 140), have always been eaten here. These warming dishes are flavoured by the generous use of sweet peppers and dried, hot chilli peppers.

The fertile central basin along the Ebro River, near Zaragoza, yields vegetables, fruit and almonds, and the olive groves produce flavoursome oil. Vegetables and oil are married in *menestra*, a slowly cooked stew that is the feature of summer meals here. Cariñena is known for its full-bodied, deeply coloured red wines.

Balearic Islands

'Floating' in the Mediterranean, the Balearic archipelago (Majorca, Minorca, Ibiza, Formentera

Spain is a predominantly Catholic country and boasts some extravagantly detailed church architecture

and Cabrera) gets most of its culinary influences from mainland Catalonia, yet the islands' food has distinctive characteristics. For visitors, however, it's necessary to travel away from the pulsating coastal tourist centres to sample traditional fare.

Islanders enjoy simply prepared food, making the most of lush vegetables and copious Mediterranean seafood, especially spiny lobsters, which are eaten by the plateful all summer long. Pork often features in meals and pork lard is used for cooking. *Sobrasada*, Majorca's sweet and peppery pork sausage, is popular all over Spain for its soft, spreadable texture, as well as its spicy flavour.

Traditional one-pot meals and hearty soups provide substance for agricultural workers and seafarers. A *sopa mallorquina*, for example, is so packed with vegetables and pork the broth is almost secondary. *Coca mallorquina* is Majorca's answer to the Italian pizza. *Coques* (the plural of *coca*), which are also enjoyed on the other islands, are easy to make at home (see page 68), and the topping can be anything from leftovers to tinned seafood or vegetables.

Grapes have been grown and wine has been produced on Majorca since Roman times, but little is exported. During the 18th-century British occupation, Minorca's wild juniper berries were put to use in gin production, which continues to this day.

Although the French always dispute this culinary legend, Spanish food historians claim mayonnaise had its origins here, rather than in France, and was eaten by the Duc de Richelieu first in Máhon, the capital of Minorca. As the legend continues, he then took the creamy egg emulsion to Paris, calling it *sauce mahonnaise*. (The fact that Catalans were

The appreciation of good food and cooking is more than just a pleasant pastime in this fiercely independent part of Spain

already making a garlic and oil emulsion that eventually had eggs incorporated to make a creamy sauce (see page 232) gives a certain amount of credibility to this version of food history.)

Minorca also produces one of the stars of Spanish cheese-making: Máhon, a pasteurized cow's milk cheese with a creamy, soft texture that hardens with age.

Basque country

The appreciation of good food and cooking is more than just a pleasant pastime in this fiercely independent part of Spain – it is said the Basques live to eat, rather than eat to live. It is also estimated there is one restaurant for every 1,000 inhabitants here, and there isn't any question of the kitchen being solely the woman's domain. All-male gastronomic societies have been established for longer than a century. The Basques are universally recognized as excellent cooks.

As in the neighbouring French Basque region, Spanish Basques cook with generous amounts of butter and cream. This, along with their own language, customs and traditions, sets them apart from other Spaniards. Try Basque Scrambled Eggs (see page 106) for an example of how local cooks handle the ever-popular Spanish eggs, or Fried Milk (see page 222) for a rich dessert. It was here that the French style of *nouvelle cuisine* made its first, tiny inroad into Spain in the form of *nueva cocina vasca*.

The Basque love of eating is well supplied by the

fresh vegetables of neighbouring Navarre, with game and wild mushrooms from the Pyrenees, seafood from the Bay of Biscay and the full-bodied wines from Navarre and La Rioja. Dishes from the region are easily identified when *a la vizcaína* appears in the title, indicating it contains onions and peppers, often specifically the chilli pepper *choricero*.

The Basques have been fishermen for generations, so the Bay of Biscay's fish and shellfish frequently appear on the table. Hake is popular, along with baby eels, spider crabs, oysters, mussels and tuna. *Bacalao* (dried salt cod) remains a favourite ingredient, a reminder of the days when the fresh catch had to be dried on board fishing vessels far from home. The simple tomato and pepper dish *bacalao a la vizcaína* is one example of the local treatment. Basques take great pleasure in serving visitors a bowl of *angulas*, tiny, thin baby eels that look as if they are swimming in broth.

This is also the part of the country where beef can take centre-stage, as many consider it the best in the country. Tapas are also a firm part of Basque culture. A full evening meal is often replaced by a couple of hours in a tapas bar, enjoying the varied selection of titbits – notoriously larger here than in other parts of Spain.

Canary Islands

These sun-drenched volcanic islands in the Atlantic Ocean – Grand Canary, Tenerife, Lanzarote, La Palma, Gomera, Hierro and Fuerteventura – are closer to Africa than the Iberian peninsula and enjoy a semi-tropical climate. As Spanish and Portuguese explorers set out in search of foreign riches during the 15th century, the Canary Islands, annexed to Spain in 1496, became an important staging post before ships set off to make, or returned from, long journeys.

Fresh produce abounds, especially large tomatoes and bananas that are exported throughout Europe.

Olive trees positively thrive in the seemingly barren wastes and searing sun of the Spanish interior

fill up agricultural workers before a day's labours, or the mixture was used to thicken soups and stews. Fresh mackerel, tuna and sardines feature in meals here, often served simply grilled with olive oil and garlic, or combined in a stew.

Sugar cane, originally introduced in the 16th century, thrives in the volcanic ash, and is made into rum, giving the islands an almost Caribbean feel.

Castilla-La Mancha & Madrid

The vast arid plateau of Castile-La Mancha in central Spain is where Cervantes' fictional Don Quixote tilted at the windmills that dot this landscape. The name La Mancha comes from the Arab word *manxa*, which means dry, and it accurately describes the sun-baked, unirrigated land – in summer the sun is unrelenting. Yet some of Spain's finest ingredients grow here: the expensive saffron (see page 33), grapes, olives and sunflowers all thrive.

Driving south from Madrid the harshness is evident as you pass through one sparsely populated dusty village after another. Food is simple, meant to provide subsistence and strength for hard labouring on the land. You will find lamb dishes and game in season. *Ollas* are meat and bean stews that provide a filling meal in a pot (see page 32). Served since the 16th century, the legendary hero Don Quixote dined on an *olla* that consisted of 'more beef than mutton'.

In a poor region like this, eggs have always featured. Hens were never expensive to keep, and the logic was that if you fed the hen, it would feed you. Tortilla (see page 42) and Eggs on Vegetables (see page 177) are examples of the inexpensive dishes from La Mancha. Vegetables are slowly stewed in *pisto manchego*, not unlike the French ratatouille. *Gazpacho manchego*, the regional bread-thickened

Favourite local dishes include *empañadas*, meat-and-vegetable pasty-like pies that make excellent snacks as well as simple meals. *Papas arraguadas*, 'Wrinkled' Potatoes (see page 84), are served with one of the piquant vinegar and pepper *mojo* sauces. The dish gets its name from the potatoes' wrinkled appearance after being boiled in salty water. *Mojo Rojo*, red Mojo Sauce (see page 84), is one of the traditional sauces; there is also a green, coriander-flavoured version, *Mojo Verde*. A dish with an ancient heritage is *gofio*, or poor man's bread, made from toasted and ground wheat, barley, cornmeal and sometimes chickpea flours. Baked into an unleavened bread, it served to

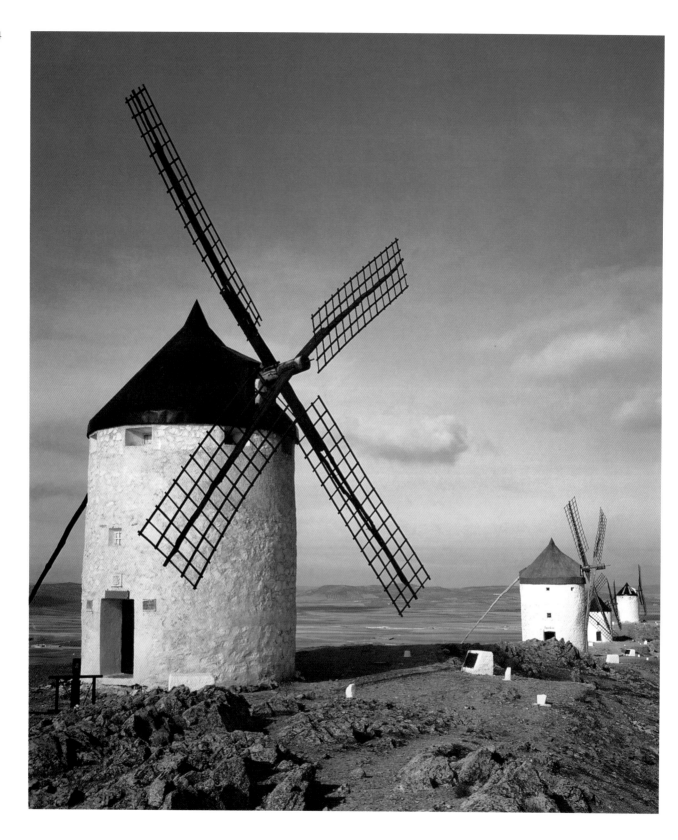

soup, provides warmth against the harsh winds that sweep across the plains, and is likely to contain whatever is available to go into the pot, be it meat or vegetables – very different indeed from the chilled gazpacho of Andalusia.

Ancient Toledo, with its crowded winding streets, is the home of Spanish marzipan (see page 225), which was 'invented' by Moorish bakers in the 13th century. Today, numerous shops sell small Nativity figures moulded out of marzipan, which are eaten all over Spain in the run-up to Christmas.

The sleepy town of Consuegra, the centre of the saffron industry (see page 33), shakes off its usual dusty appearance at the end of October with the annual Fiesta de la Rosa del Azafrán, or saffron festival, when the saffron harvest is finished.

La Mancha also contains Spain's largest wine region, with the best wine produced around Valdepeñas. Most of the region's production, however, is *vino comun*, or table wine for everyday drinking.

In cosmopolitan Madrid, though, food is more lavish and lighter, reflecting the capital's historical links with royal courts. Leisurely meals are as much about enjoyment as simply fuelling the body, and the numerous tapas bars around the Plaza Mayor provide pleasant meeting places for *madrileños* and tourists alike.

For a taste of traditional Madrid cuisine, try *cocido madrileño* (Madrid hotpot), a one-pot feast served over three courses. The meal begins with the richly flavoured broth containing cooked rice. Next, the vegetables of the dish – cabbage, carrots, potatoes and tender chickpeas – are presented. Finally, it is time for the selection of meats that have been simmered until meltingly tender. A typical combination might be beef, chorizo sausage, pork

Spain's vast, arid central plateau, with its famous windmills, is the home of simply cooked meat and bean dishes

La Mancha also contains Spain's largest wine region, with the best wine produced around Valdepeñas

shoulder, chicken and tiny meatballs. Little wonder that the three courses are referred to as the *sato*, *caballo* and *rey*, or jack, queen and king, as the dish is said to increase in nobility as the meal progresses.

Castilla y Leon and La Rioja

Gastronomically, these regions are linked because of strong historical and geographical ties. This is the land of *asados*, or roasted meats. For many, the best, tenderest meat in Spain comes from here, especially around Segovia, where the most desirable are the *cochinillo* (suckling pig) and *lechazo* (milk-fed baby lamb), which have been roasted here since the 15th century. They are butchered at around three weeks, and the cooked meat is said to be so tender it can be cut with the edge of a plate. The conical adobe ovens traditionally used to spit-roast these delicacies over burning vine clippings (*hornos de asar*) were found originally in bakeries, as most farmhouse ovens – where they even existed – were too small to roast whole animals.

Spaniards almost always eat bread with meals, but here a meal simply isn't considered complete if bread isn't served. For centuries pilgrims bound for Santiago de Compostela have stopped in Astogra to relish the rolls (*mantecades*) said to 'bulk large in the hand and light on the stomach'. Perfect partners for the bread are the simple pulse and vegetable stews that were once the mainstay of daily diets. *Sopa de ajo*, or garlic soup, once a peasant broth of garlic, eggs and bread, now appears on restaurant menus everywhere.

The Andalusian custom of preserving foods *en escabeche*, in vinegar, was embraced and perfected

Cooks in other parts of Spain must look with envy at the riches from the Mediterranean and Pyrenees that Catalan cooks choose from

here, and everything from vegetables to game gets the treatment. You can experience the fresh taste of this preserving style with Pickled Mackerel (see page 53) or Veal with Pickled Vegetables (see page 139).

Ribera del Duero, the wine region of Castilla y Léon located along the Duero River that winds its way from Portugal to Madrid, produces predominantly fine red wines. Fertile soils and mountainous terrain combine to make La Rioja, which takes its name from the Oja River (Rìo Oja), the home of the full-bodied red and white Rioja wines, some of the finest in Spain. Wines have been produced here since Roman times, but were undistinguished until the late 19th century when phylloxera wiped out the French vines, and Bordeaux winemakers moved to the region.

Surprisingly, wines do not often feature much in cooking, except the popular dessert of fruit poached in wine. A recipe with *a la riojana* in the title does not mean that the dish includes wine, rather that peppers are an important ingredient, because this is the centre of Spain's pepper-growing farms. (The peppers Spanish cooks use will always be the long, pointed ones, which are infinitely sweeter and more flavoursome than the bell-shaped peppers produced under glass in northern Europe. Look out for this pointed variety, described as Mediterranean-style peppers, in most supermarkets.) The full-bodied and simple food from here often includes beans and peppers, such as in Lamb Stew with Chickpeas (see page 144). Asparagus and cardoons are grown in La Rioja too, and *menesta riojana* is a simmered stew

of vegetables. A typical flavouring of the Riojan dishes here comes from the combination of fruit, garlic, olive oil, onions, nuts and tomatoes that grow throughout the region.

Catalonia

Barcelona, Spain's largest city and the capital of this independently minded region, is considered by many also to be Spain's gastronomic capital. Stay away from harbourside tourist restaurants and you will eat and drink well here for less than in most other major European cities. Catalan cuisine is not fancy or heavily sauced, instead relying on the flavours of fresh, seasonal ingredients. It is an ancient cuisine, with Can Culleretes restaurant, supposedly the oldest in Barcelona, dating from 1786. And a Catalan is credited with writing the oldest published Spanish cookbook – in the early 1500s.

Catalan cooking is distinguished by four classic sauces that provide the backbone of most cooked dishes. *Sofregit* is slow-cooked onions and tomatoes, and sometimes garlic, used at the start of cooking; *picada* is a mixture of fried bread, garlic, olive oil and nuts pounded with a pestle and mortar used to thicken and flavour many dishes; *samfaina* is the all-purpose Catalan version of ratatouille that is just as often stirred into stews as a flavouring as served on its own as a vegetable dish; *Allioli* (see page 232) is a garlic-flavoured mayonnaise that is served with everything from fried potatoes to seafood stews. Some food writers argue that Romesco Sauce (see page 233), a mixture of toasted nuts, the dried local *romesco* chilli and tomatoes, which accompanies local seafood dishes, should be added to the list.

Cooks in other parts of Spain must look with envy at the riches from the Mediterranean and Pyrenees that Catalan cooks choose from. Their ingredients range from Alpine-like mushrooms to the freshest just-caught crustaceans, and plenty of cereals,

Barcelona and its port, with the tree-lined avenue called Las Ramblas, meaning the walkway

page 169), which comprises pieces of cod served on tender young spinach flavoured with raisins and pine kernels, reflects the Arab style of using dried fruit in savoury recipes. *Fidenà*, a seafood casserole with thin pieces of pasta called *fidens*, is a popular restaurant dish, but difficult to master at home. *Romesco de pescado* is one of the many versions of seafood stew, this one made with white beans and flavoured by a good dollop of Romesco Sauce (see page 233) as it finishes cooking.

Yet, even with all the fresh ingredients on offer, Catalan cooks are masters at preparing *bacalao* (dried salt cod). A quintessential Catalan speciality is *Esqueixada*, a raw salt cod salad lightly dressed with extra virgin olive oil and vinegar and garnished with finely diced tomatoes (see page 89).

Grilling, especially barbecuing, is a popular method of cooking, ideal for both meat and seafood. The arrival of spring is heralded with grilled *calçots* (spring onions) for dipping in Romesco Sauce.

Cantabria

The Bay of Biscay offers an abundance of fresh tuna, bonito, sardines and anchovies to the cooks of this small region along the Costa Verde (Green Coast), while inland waters supply salmon and trout.

Santander is a holiday destination for many Spaniards and northern Europeans and the entire region is dotted with simple, family-run seafood restaurants. You'll also find plenty of grilled meats on the menu. Orchards provide the apples that are used in sweet tarts and local cakes.

A large dairy industry here means milk is used extensively in cooking, and the rich desserts include Fried Milk (see page 222) and creamy rice puddings, such as *Arroz con Leche* (see page 196).

vegetables, fruit, olives and oil, pork and game. (Pork fat replaces olive oil in traditional Catalan recipes.) And, of course, as Barcelona is one of the Mediterranean's major ports, produce and goods from other countries enter Spain here, increasing what is on offer. One look at the covered La Boqueria market illustrates just what an international cornucopia Catalans enjoy.

The supply of fresh Mediterranean fish is varied and abundant. Black Rice (see page 122) is a regional speciality of squid and rice, flavoured and coloured with the squid's black ink. Cod with Spinach (see

28

Extremadura

Village life can seem almost timeless in this sparsely populated 'extreme and hard' land, bordering Portugal. The mountain farms produce some of Spain's most gastronomically valued pork products. Black Iberian pigs graze on nuts and acorns from the stone oak and cork trees, which are said to flavour the leg meat that is salt-cured and dried, when it becomes the delicious *jamón iberico* (see page 32). The meat is cured in salt then left to mature in cellars for up to two years. Some of the finest comes from Montánchez.

Nothing is wasted, and the remainder of the pig is combined with the locally produced paprika to make what some consider to be the best chorizo in Spain.

Relaxed social events, such as this alfresco *performance, are very much part of the Spanish way of life*

Paprika production is big here, and *pimentón de la Vera* is the *denominación de origen* that guarantees its quality.

Galicia

The Moorish culinary influence is less evident in Galicia than other parts of Spain, and the light Mediterranean cooking might as well be from a different country.

Nestled in Spain's northwest corner, Galicia takes a battering from the fierce Atlantic winds. It has the longest coastline of any Spanish region, with Europe's largest port at Vigo, so shellfish and seafood are common ingredients in its distinctive cuisine. The local clams, oysters and scallops are renowned, and Atlantic fish such as flounder, mackerel and sea bass are also popular. The local northern version of the more famous Mediterranean fish stew, *bouillabaisse*, is *caldereta de pescado*.

The scallop shell, symbol of St James the Apostle, is carried by pilgrims who arrive at the cathedral town of Santiago de Compostela, as they have since the Middle Ages. St James is the patron saint of Spain, so the National Day celebrations in this medieval town on 25 July are lively and elaborate. There is plenty to eat throughout the day, culminating with a slice of the local Almond Tart (see page 218).

Lush, green pastures mean meat, especially pork and game, is enjoyed here. As in Portugal, shellfish and meat are combined in simmered casseroles, such as clams with pork. Galician cooks also use butter and lard to add a richness to cooking that is not evident in the regions that use olive oil.

Pimientos de Padrón, the tiny green peppers that Spaniards munch deep-fried (see page 49), are grown here. Tetilla, a breast-shaped cow's milk cheese, also comes from Galicia.

The dry white wines produced in Galicia's vineyards make perfect partners for the shellfish recipes, and the bone-dry reds are ideal to complement the rich meat dishes of the region.

The Levant

This fertile region, along the Mediterranean, which comprises the provinces of Valencia, Alicante and Murcia between Andalusia and Catalonia, grows the fruit and vegetables the rest of Spain and much of Europe enjoy. Valencia is rice country. Rice paddies around Lake Albufera, south of the city of Valencia, produce the tonnes of short-grain rice that feed most of the country. Calasparra rice, from Murcia,

Paella ... is unbeatable for adding a Spanish flavour when you are feeding a crowd

considered by many the finest, is grown on terraces that were built by the Moors in the 12th century.

La paella is the best-known dish of the region, with references to it in travellers' journals from the 14th century. This classic rice dish, traditionally cooked outdoors as a meatless Lenten meal, gets its name from the shallow two-handled pan it is cooked in, a *paella*, which comes from the Latin word for a 'pan'. Visit any Spanish market and you will find paella pans on sale that range in size from 30 cm/ 12 inches to several metres wide, large enough to feed an entire village. Paella pans, with their sloping sides, are specifically designed to expose a wide surface area so the liquid evaporates before the rice becomes overcooked, and to ensure even heat distribution over a fire. They are available from cookware shops, but you can also use a flameproof earthenware or cast-iron casserole, or a large, shallow frying pan with an ovenproof handle.

Paella is adaptable to whatever ingredients are available, whether seafood, meat, poultry or vegetables. The dish is unbeatable for adding a Spanish flavour when you are feeding a crowd, but it takes time and attention to make a good paella. (If you want a quick alternative, try the Rice with Chorizo and Prawns recipe on page 125.)

Another rice speciality, *all-i-pebre*, or garlic and peppers, gives no hint of its main ingredient of eels. Fisherman once prepared *arroz a banda*, or rice and seafood, to eat on board fishing vessels, but now it seems as if every restaurant along the coast prepares this saffron- and fish stock-flavoured dish, which is eaten in two courses – rice first and then the fish

The elegant palm groves of Elche are unique in Europe

with Garlic Mayonnaise (see page 232). The vast salt marshes in the region give rise to fish dishes baked in salt, which creates a thick 'container' to seal in all moisture and freshness. During baking the coating becomes so solid the salt casing has to be broken with a mallet at the table.

The combination of rice and beans in *moros y cristianos*, or Moors and Christians (see page 182), is a legacy from ancient wars when the region was controlled by Arabs before El Cid won it back for the Christians.

Valencia is also where oranges reign supreme, and find their way into many savoury and sweet dishes; most of the country's lemons are grown here, too. Valencia oranges are one of Spain's major export items. The combination of potatoes and orange is recognized as *a la valenciana*, and the tradition of cooking seafood in orange juice goes back to the Middle Ages. Try the Orange and Fennel Salad (see page 109) for a taste of the region.

Milk is extracted from a tiny tuber that grows here called the *chufa*, or tiger nut, to make a mild-tasting drink called *horchata*.

Murcia is the land of juicy red tomatoes, large globe artichokes, other tender green vegetables and succulent fruit, all grown in the semi-arid land away from the coast with the extensive irrigation systems developed by the Moors. This is where you'll find colourful salads utilizing the variety of produce, such as Grilled Pepper Salad (see page 178) and Tuna and Bean Salad (see page 181). The tiny capers that add a piquant flavour to so many Mediterranean dishes grow here, too, for packing in salt or oil. On the back of such extensive agriculture, the region is also one of the major centres of Spain's vegetable canning

industry – one look at the supermarket shelves confirms what a significant industry this is.

The elegant palm groves of Elche are unique in Europe, and provide the main ingredient for sweet-meats, such as Dates Stuffed with Spanish Marzipan (see page 225).

Traditional seafood recipes have always featured along this sunny Mediterranean coast, with hake, tuna, grey mullet and giant prawns plentiful. Yet, even with so much fresh seafood, salt-cured blue-fin tuna (*mojama*) is a local speciality.

Navarre

Southern Navarre nestles between La Rioja and Aragón, so pepper-flavoured lamb *chilindróns* are popular here, flavoured with the *del choriceros* or *del pico* peppers that flourish on the banks of the Ebro River. Lamb and pork are the meats of choice, as the beef is often destined for the bullring, rather than tables. At the daring running of the bulls each July in Pamplona, *pastel de conejo*, a rabbit pie, is a regular feature of evening meals.

The white asparagus that is grown here is eaten throughout Spain as a spring delicacy. Humble *migas*, fried bread cubes, have made their way from peasant mountain cooking to tapas bars everywhere, but here they are also served with chocolate sauce or grapes. Another regional use of chocolate is to cook game birds in a dark chocolate sauce.

Restaurant menus often feature *truchas a la navarra*, river trout marinated in the local robust red wines with herbs and spices, and then poached in the marinade. Mountain shepherds, though, simply fry their freshly caught trout in pans over open fires of wild herb cuttings, adding diced *serrano* ham for extra flavouring.

Hotels and apartment blocks hug Spain's beaches to accommodate the influx of tourists and holiday-makers

In the Spanish kitchen

Almonds (almendras) These rich, creamy nuts feature in almost every aspect of Spanish cooking, savoury and sweet. The Moors introduced almond trees, planting the first groves near Granada in Andalusia. At their simplest, a plate of almonds is a tapas. Ground almonds are used as a thickening agent or as a replacement for some flour in desserts, but their starring role in Spanish cuisine is in confections, especially turrón. Almonds quickly become rancid because of their high fat content: store them in a cool, dark place, say the fridge – even the freezer. Buy unblanched almonds as the skins help prevent the nuts drying out (see page 50 for how to blanch almonds).

Cheese (queso) *Manchego*, a renowned sheep's milk cheese from La Mancha, is believed by many foreigners to be Spain's only cheese, but the choice is vast, with traditional cheeses made from cow's, sheep's and goat's milks, or from a mixture of milks. Some food writers claim Spain has more individual cheeses than neighbouring France, although many are regional and not exported, or even available in other parts of the country.

Chickpeas (garbanzos) Spanish explorers introduced these slightly nutty, rich, round pulses from the New World. In their dried form they need overnight soaking and boiling before they become tender and edible, but Spanish cooks save time by buying them in cans or on market stalls *en remojo* – soaked and ready for cooking.

Chilli peppers (pimientos chili) Heat in a Spanish dish will most likely be provided by red chilli peppers, but their use is more judicious than is often assumed. The robust mountain dishes from the northwest are flavoured with tiny *guindilla* peppers – the hottest of all. The sweet, but still with heat, romesco peppers are used in Catalonia's Romesco Sauce (see page 233), but as these are not widely available, *ñora* (or *nyora*), peppers are a

good substitute. The *choricero* chilli provides the flavour and red-orange colour of chorizo sausages.

Chorizo sausage (chorizo) Spain has a wonderful and varied selection of cured and raw sausages, of which one of the best known is chorizo. All chorizos are made from pork and contain paprika made from the *choricero* chilli pepper, but beyond that the variety seems endless. Chorizos can be thick, thin, smoked, unsmoked, mildly flavoured or spicy, and contain varying amounts of fat.

Garlic (ajo) Desserts are probably the only Spanish dishes that do not include this pungent vegetable. The bleak, dusty plains of La Mancha are home to Spain's garlic-growing industry. Buy firm, plump heads with a tight, white outer skin, and store in a cool, dry place. The bulb should remain fresh for a month, but once a head has been broken into, the individual cloves will start to dry out and should be used within 10 days.

Ham (jamón) In a country where the pig is king, hams have been produced for at least 2,000 years. *Serrano* ham is a generic term for the salt-cured, breeze-dried leg meat of pigs from mountainous regions. The most prized hams are those made from black Iberian pigs, especially around Jabugo, Lèrida, Montánchez, Teruel and Trevélez. A long maturation period is one reason the best ham is expensive; the other is that it is often hand-sliced. Less expensive ham is used in cooking, but the finest is served raw as a tapas. Italian prosciutto is an acceptable substitute. Cooked ham is *jamón cocido*.

Hotpot stews (cocidos) These are rich stews that feature in most regions, the ultimate being *cocido madrileño*, an enormous feast of three courses (see page 25). *Olla*, meaning 'pot', is another name for these one-pot meals.

Olive oil (aceite de oliva) This is the most important ingredient in the Spanish kitchen. It is used in all types of cooking, as a flavouring and as a preservative, even as the main source of fat in many baking recipes, where other cuisines use animal fats. Spain is the largest olive oil producer in the world. Strict labelling regulations cover the olive oil grades, which are determined by the process used to extract the oil and the amount of oleic acid. Extra virgin (*aceite de oliva virgen extra*) is the finest quality from the first cold pressing. Virgin (*aceite de oliva virgen*) is also cold pressed, but not as refined as extra virgin. Oil simply labelled 'olive oil' (*aceite de oliva*) is a blend of virgin and refined olive oils. It is exported, but more difficult to find than the extra virgin. There is little point in using the finest extra virgin oils for frying, as the subtle flavours are destroyed by intense heat: save them for salad dressings and marinades.

Olives (azeitunas) Spaniards are spoilt for choice when it comes to olives, and a bowl of olives is often served as the most simple tapas. Most other fruit contains large amounts of water; olives have oil. Over 50 varieties are grown, and over half those for eating, not pressing, come from Andalusia. Varieties include: *aragón*, small, smooth-skinned pale black with a hint of pink; *arbequiña*, tiny, round, and pale green; *cacereña*, small, black, with firm flesh; *gordal*, very large, green, with a full flavour; and *manzanilla* (or Seville), small, green but fat, meaty and often stuffed with anchovies, pimentos or tiny olives.

Paprika (pimentón) The orange-red colour and sweet-to-hot earthy flavour of paprika finds its way into many Spanish dishes and ingredients. Paprika is the finely ground powder of dried red peppers; the degree of heat and intensity of colour depends on the variety of pepper. Hungarians are also major producers of paprika, but the Spanish variety is usually milder and slightly sweeter, although you will find some very hot Spanish paprika.

Rice (arroz) The short-grain rice grown in the coastal plains of the Levant is a staple ingredient found in most Spanish kitchens. It is the essential ingredient for Paella (see page 112), as well as other rice preparations. Traditional Spanish rice cooking is unique in that the rice is neither covered nor stirred during cooking, resulting in dishes that are quite different from long-grain pilafs or creamy risottos, for example. All rice recipes, except Rice with Chorizo and Prawns (see page 124), have been tested with Calasparra rice, from Murcia. You can substitute the short-grain rice sold in supermarkets as 'Paella Rice'; short-grain pudding rice and risotto rice make the result too mushy. Rice with Chorizo and Prawns uses the new quick-cooking variety.

Saffron (azafrán) The golden hue and distinctive flavour of saffron is unmistakable in such classic Spanish dishes as Paella and Catalan Fish Stew (see page 156). Saffron was introduced by the Moors when they conquered Spain in the early 8th century. It is made from the stigmas of the crocus and is the world's most expensive spice, because the labour-intensive process of removing the dusky red stigmas from the crocus plants (*Crocus sativus*) must be done by hand. It takes up to 75,000 stigmas to produce 450 g/1 lb saffron. Today, sleepy villages in La Mancha produce an overwhelming amount of the world's supply. Harvesting the 'red gold' takes place in October and the entire population of a village will become involved. Once the stigmas have been collected they are quickly toasted, after which, properly stored in an airtight container, the aroma will stay fresh for up to three years. Turmeric is often given as an acceptable, less expensive substitute for saffron, but although it gives a lovely golden colour, its flavour and aroma are not at all similar.

Turron (turrón) This honey-flavoured delicacy is similar to nougat. Its centre of production since the times of the Moors has been Jijona, in the hills above Alicante. The two traditional versions, soft (*blando*) and hard (*duro*), have changed little over the centuries.

TAPAS & STARTERS

One of the most pleasurable aspects of any visit to Spain is sampling the amazing array of tapas served in every village, town or city. The preparation, eating and enjoyment of tapas is a uniquely Spanish experience. Italians have *antipasti*; the French enjoy *hors d'oeuvres*; and a Greek *mezze* can consist of a dazzling display of appetizers, but no other culture has anything quite like tapas.

Tapas are an institution everywhere in Spain. These are titbits of food for nibbling with drinks while chatting with friends, and range from a simple bowl of olives or almonds to more elaborate stuffed peppers or golden tortilla.

Tapas can be made with seafood, meat, poultry, eggs and vegetables, and served hot or chilled. As with most things Spanish, few conventions apply universally, but tapas bars usually open from lunchtime for several hours and then again in the evening when the work day finishes. For someone from Barcelona, for example, stopping off for tapas with colleagues will be a prelude to going home or on to a restaurant for the evening meal, whereas someone from Madrid might eat enough tapas to forgo another meal.

In most of the country the daily selection of tapas is displayed on a bar and a waiter puts your selection on a plate, for eating either standing up or seated at the bar or a table. In northern Spain, however, you help yourself and the bill is settled at the end, calculated on the number of small plates, cocktail sticks or small wooden forks used to spear bite-size titbits like grilled scallops or snails in oil. In Barcelona and other large cities long 'fast-food' tapas bars thrive, with photographs of the range of tapas available on paper placemats — ideal for non-Spanish-speaking tourists, who can simply point and order!

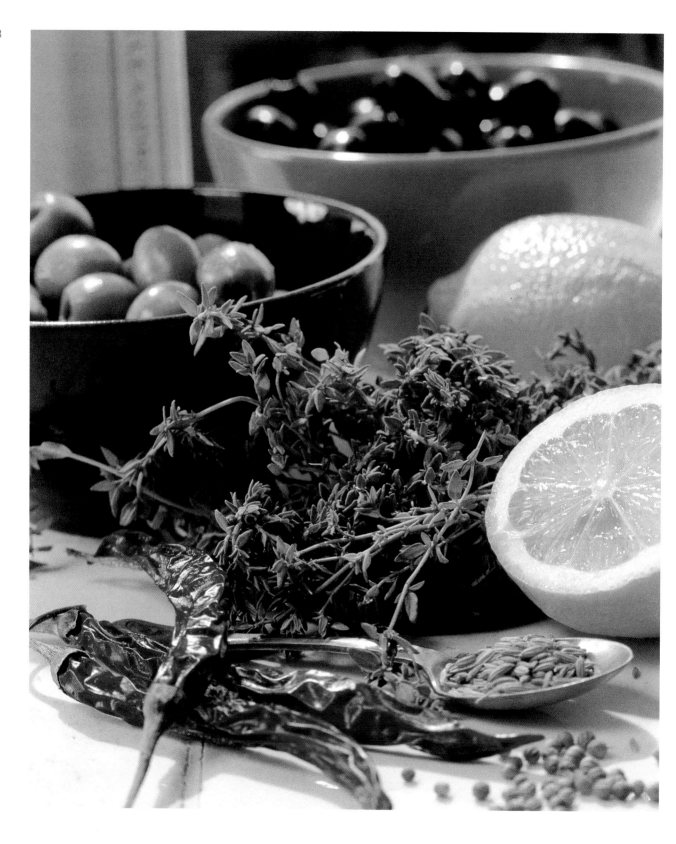

The word 'tapas' means a lid or cover, and it is thought tapas got their name from the days when a slice of bread covered with ham or cheese was placed on top of a wine or sherry glass to keep flies out while serving weary travellers on horseback. The price of simple tapas was once included in the cost of drinks, but that tradition, sadly, has all but died out.

The vast array of tapas fits within different categories. *Cosas de picar*, meaning little things to nibble, are finger food, such as Marinated Olives (see page 47), Paprika-spiced Almonds (see page 50), Deep-fried Green Chillies (see page 49), slices of Spanish Tortilla (see page 42) and Salads on Bread (see page 93). *Pinchos* are slightly more substantial and speared with cocktail sticks, such as Chorizo and Mushroom Kebabs (see page 74), Feisty Potatoes (see page 86), Chicken Livers with Sherry Glaze (see page 78) and Tiny Meatballs with Tomato Sauce (see page 77). *Cazuelas* are the distinctive small,

It is thought tapas got their name from the days when a slice of bread covered with ham or cheese was placed on top of a wine or sherry glass to keep flies out

brown earthenware dishes used by cooks all over Spain, so the tapas served in those dishes are likewise called *cazuelas*. These include Garlic Prawns with Lemon and Parsley (see page 64) and Broad Beans with Ham (see page 81). *Raciones* are the more filling tapas, such as small kebabs, a selection of which will easily substitute for a meal.

Overleaf *Spain is so much more than sun and sandy beaches and exhibits an immense diversity of landscape*

spanish tortilla
tortilla española

There is hardly a tapas bar in Spain that doesn't serve this simple, but delicious, set, thick omelette, and there can't be many Spanish cooks who don't make it look effortless as they turn out a golden tortilla. Generations ago it was said that country girls could improve their chance of marrying early by making an excellent tortilla.

This classic recipe, with only the simple ingredients of eggs, potatoes and onion, is also known as tortilla española. *Other tortilla names, however, give a clue to where they come from and what they include:* tortilla murciana *contains red peppers and tomatoes;* tortilla a la catalana *features the local* butifarra *sausage and beans;* tortilla de berenjenas *is an Andalusian aubergine version.*

MAKES 8–10 SLICES

125 ml/4 fl oz olive oil

600 g/1 lb 5 oz potatoes, peeled and sliced thinly

1 large onion, sliced thinly

6 large eggs

salt and pepper

flat-leaved parsley, to garnish

1 Heat a 25-cm/10-inch frying pan, preferably non-stick, over a high heat. Add the oil and heat. Reduce the heat, then add the potatoes and onion and cook for 15–20 minutes until the potatoes are tender.

2 Beat the eggs in a large bowl and season generously with salt and pepper. Drain the potatoes and onion through a sieve over a heatproof bowl to reserve the oil. Very gently stir the vegetables into the eggs; set aside for 10 minutes.

3 Use a wooden spoon or spatula to remove any crusty bits stuck to the base of the frying pan. Reheat the frying pan over a medium-high heat with 4 tablespoons of the reserved oil. Add the egg mixture and smooth the surface, pressing the potatoes and onions into an even layer.

4 Cook for about 5 minutes, shaking the frying pan occasionally, until the base is set. Use a spatula to loosen the side of the tortilla. Place a large plate over the top and carefully invert the frying pan and plate together* so the tortilla drops onto the plate.

5 Add 1 tablespoon of the remaining reserved oil to the frying pan and swirl around. Carefully slide the tortilla back into the frying pan, cooked side up. Run the spatula around the tortilla, to tuck in the edge.

6 Continue cooking for about 3 minutes until the eggs are set and the base is golden brown. Remove the frying pan from the heat and slide the tortilla onto a plate. Leave to stand for at least 5 minutes before cutting. Serve warm or at room temperature.

*cook's tip

If you are uncomfortable about inverting the tortilla, finish cooking it under a medium-high grill, about 10 cm/4 inches from the heat source, until the runny egg mixture on top is set. The tortilla will not, however, have its characteristic 'rounded' edge.

oven-baked tortilla
tortilla al horno

In Madrid's tapas bars you could be served this simply in 2.5-cm/1-inch squares with cocktail sticks for picking up, while in other parts of Spain the squares might be presented on bread slices.

MAKES 48 PIECES

olive oil

1 large garlic clove, crushed

4 spring onions, white and green parts chopped finely

1 green pepper, cored, deseeded and diced finely

1 red pepper, cored, deseeded and diced finely

175 g/6 oz potato, boiled, peeled and diced

5 large eggs

100 ml/3^1/$_2$ fl oz soured cream

175 g/6 oz freshly grated Spanish Roncal cheese, or use Cheddar or Parmesan

3 tbsp snipped fresh chives

salt and pepper

1 Line an 18 x 25-cm/7 x 10-inch baking tray with foil and brush with the oil; set aside.

2 Put a little oil, the garlic, spring onions and peppers in a frying pan and cook over a medium heat, stirring, for about 10 minutes until the onions are soft, but not brown. Remove from the heat and leave to cool. Stir in the potato.

3 Beat the eggs, soured cream, cheese and chives together in a large bowl. Stir the cooled vegetables into the bowl and season with salt and pepper to taste.

4 Pour the mixture into the baking tray and smooth over the top. Bake in an oven preheated to 190°C/375°F/Gas Mark 5 for 30–40 minutes until golden brown, puffed, and set in the centre. Remove from the oven and leave to cool and set. Run a spatula around the edge, then invert onto a chopping board, browned side up; peel off the foil. If the surface looks a little runny, put it under a medium grill to dry out.

5 Leave to cool completely. Trim the edges if necessary, then cut into 48 squares. Serve on a platter with wooden cocktail sticks, or secure each square to a slice of bread.

tomato bread
pa amb tomàquet

It is most unusual to have a meal in Barcelona that doesn't begin with Pa amb Tomàquet, *whether you are in a tapas bar, restaurant or a private home. This is one of the classics of the region.*

sliced bread or French loaf

tomatoes

garlic, optional

olive oil, optional

1 At its simplest, slices of bread are simply rubbed with half a fresh juicy tomato. If the bread is soft, you can toast it first. Other options are to flavour it with garlic, or drizzle olive oil over the top.

variation

For a more substantial snack, serve *pan con tomate* with a plate of thinly sliced serrano ham and Manchego cheese, and let guests assemble open sandwiches.

marinated olives

azeitunas aliñadas

A Spanish cook is just as likely to buy marinated olives as to prepare his or her own, as the choice is so vast with endless flavour combinations.

Markets and supermarkets always offer a huge selection of flavoured olives, along with other vegetables, such as chillies and the long, sweet, Mediterranean-style peppers. When you don't have so much choice, however, a jar of these is handy to have in the cupboard, to serve with drinks.

FILLS A 500-ML/18-FL OZ PRESERVING JAR

175 g/6 oz green pimiento-stuffed Spanish olives in
   brine, rinsed

175 g/6 oz black Spanish olives in brine, rinsed

55 g/2 oz grilled and peeled pepper (see page 74),
   sliced thinly

2 thin lemon slices

2 sprigs of fresh thyme

1 bay leaf

1 dried red chilli

1/2 tsp fennel seeds

1/2 tsp coriander seeds, cracked lightly

extra virgin olive oil*

1 Place the olives, pepper strips, lemon slices, thyme, bay leaf, chilli and fennel and coriander seeds in a 500-ml/18-fl oz preserving jar, making sure the ingredients are well mixed. Pour over enough oil to cover. Seal the jar and set aside at room temperature for at least 2 weeks before using.

*cook's tips

Do not add sliced garlic to an oil marinade such as this, because of the possibility of botulism infection. If you want a garlic flavour, use a commercially prepared garlic-flavoured olive oil instead.

If you store the marinade in the fridge, the oil will become cloudy, but it clears again as it returns to room temperature.

olives and anchovies
azeitunas y boquerones

You could be served this stylish tapas with drinks in a fashionable Barcelona restaurant. It is simplicity itself, and a chance to use your best extra virgin olive oil, the flavour of which is lost in cooking. In fact, this tapas is a wonderful example of Spanish fast food — all the ingredients will be in the kitchen cupboard. Another quick and easy example is to secure a marinated anchovy fillet around an olive. Precise quantities are not important.

**seasoned anchovy fillets packed in vegetable oil
(found in Spanish food shops)**
Marinated Olives (see page 47)
small white pickled onions
extra virgin olive oil

1 Separate the anchovies into individual fillets, then arrange on a plate with the olives and onions.

2 Drizzle with the best extra virgin olive oil and serve with plenty of cocktail sticks to spear the individual ingredients while you chat over drinks.

deep-fried green chillies 49
pimientos fritos

Any sweet or hot chilli peppers can be quickly deep-fried, and the stubby pimientos de Padrón, *from the vegetable gardens south of Santiago de Compostela in Galicia, make an intriguing tapas to nibble with drinks when fried whole. You will find them in Spanish foodstores and some supermarkets sold in 250-g/9-oz bags. They have a fresh chilli taste, without much heat – except every bag seems to include one searingly hot chilli, and you won't know which it is until you bite into it.*

EACH BAG OF CHILLIES SERVES 4–6
olive oil
sweet or hot green chillies
sea salt

1 Heat 7.5 cm/3 inches of oil in a heavy-based saucepan until it reaches 190°C/375°F, or until a day-old cube of bread turns brown in 30 seconds.

2 Rinse the chillies and pat them very dry with kitchen paper. Drop them in the hot oil for no longer than 20 seconds until they turn bright green and the skins blister.

3 Remove with a slotted spoon and drain well on crumpled kitchen paper. Sprinkle with sea salt and serve at once.

variation
For a more elaborate tapas, top a thin slice of bread with a fried egg, yolk side up. Secure the egg to the bread by skewering the set white to the bread with a cocktail stick with a fried *pimiento de Padrón* on it.

paprika-spiced almonds
almendras al pimentón

Almonds in a seemingly endless variety of
preparations are a popular Spanish snack with
drinks. They are often included in a selection of tapas
or served with sherry or wine in many wine or
cocktail bars. Sometimes the almonds will be simply
blanched without any extra flavourings, while other
times they will be fried in olive oil and sprinkled with
coarse sea salt or coated with very finely ground
salt. This version adds the piquant flavour of paprika.
These almonds will keep for up to 3 days in an
airtight container.

MAKES 500 G/1 LB 2 OZ; SERVES 4–6

1¹/₂ tbsp coarse sea salt

¹/₂ tsp smoked sweet Spanish paprika, or hot paprika,
to taste

500 g/1 lb 2 oz blanched almonds*

extra virgin olive oil

1 Put the sea salt and paprika in a mortar and grind
with the pestle to a fine powder, or use a mini spice
blender (the amount is too small to process in a
full-size processor).

2 Place the almonds on a baking sheet and toast in
a preheated oven, 200°C/400°F/Gas Mark 6, for
8–10 minutes, stirring occasionally, until golden brown
and giving off a toasted aroma: watch carefully after
7 minutes because they burn quickly. Immediately pour
into a heatproof bowl.

3 Drizzle over about 1 tablespoon of oil and stir to
ensure all the nuts are lightly and evenly coated;
add extra oil, if necessary. Sprinkle with the salt and
paprika mixture and stir again. Transfer to a small bowl
and serve at room temperature.

*cook's tip

It is best, and more economical, to buy unblanched
almonds and blanch them as and when required,
because they begin to dry out as soon as the thin,
brown skin is removed. Put the unblanched almonds
in a heatproof bowl. Pour over boiling water and leave
to stand for 1 minute. Drain well, then pat dry and slip
off the skins.

pickled mackerel
caballa en escabeche   53

SERVES 4–6

8 fresh mackerel fillets

300 ml/^{1}/$_2$ pint extra virgin olive oil

2 large red onions, sliced thinly

2 carrots, peeled and sliced

2 bay leaves

2 garlic cloves, sliced thinly

2 dried red chillies

1 fennel bulb, halved and sliced thinly

300 ml/^{1}/$_2$ pint sherry vinegar

1^1/$_2$ tbsp coriander seeds

salt and pepper

toasted French bread slices, to serve

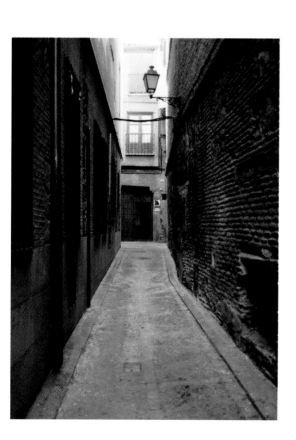

1 Place the mackerel fillets, skin side up, on a grill rack and brush lightly with a little of the oil. Grill under a medium-high grill, about 10 cm/4 inches from the heat source, for 4–6 minutes until the skins become brown and crispy and the flesh flakes easily; set aside.

2 Heat the remaining oil in a large frying pan. Add the onions and fry for about 5 minutes until soft, but not brown. Add the remaining ingredients and simmer for 10 minutes, or until the carrots are tender.

3 Flake the mackerel flesh into large pieces, removing the skin and tiny bones. Place the mackerel pieces in a preserving jar and pour over the onion, carrot and fennel mixture. (The jar should accommodate everything packed in quite tightly with the minimum air gap at the top once the vegetable mixture has been poured in.) Leave to cool completely, then cover tightly and chill for at least 24 hours and up to 5 days. Serve the pieces of mackerel on toasted slices of French bread with a little of the oil drizzled over.

Alternatively, serve the mackerel and its pickled vegetables as a first-course salad.

variation
This pickling brine is equally delicious with grilled cod or hake fillets, grilled and shelled mussels, or pan-fried tuna or swordfish steaks.

Tapas bars and restaurants serving the real food of Spain are often tucked away from the obvious tourist haunts

fried pickled monkfish

rape escabechado frito

SERVES 4–6

600 g/1¹⁄₄ lb monkfish

600–900 ml/1–1¹⁄₂ pints extra virgin olive oil

6 shallots, sliced thinly

2 carrots, peeled and sliced

1 fennel bulb, halved and sliced thinly

2 bay leaves

2 garlic cloves, sliced thinly

¹⁄₂ tsp dried chilli flakes, or to taste

300 ml/¹⁄₂ pint white wine vinegar

salt and pepper

1¹⁄₂ tbsp coriander seeds

lemon wedges, to serve

for the batter

150 g/5 oz plain flour, plus about 4 tablespoons
   extra for dusting

¹⁄₂ tsp salt

1 egg, separated

about 200 ml/7 fl oz beer

1 tbsp olive oil

1 Remove the thin membrane covering the monkfish, then rinse the tail and pat it dry. Cut the tail lengthways on either side of the central bone, then remove the bone and discard. Cut the monkfish flesh crossways into 1-cm/¹⁄₂-inch slices.

2 Heat 4 tablespoons of the oil in a large skillet over a moderate heat. Add as many monkfish slices as will fit in a single layer and fry for 2 minutes. Turn over and continue for about 4 minutes, or until the slices are just cooked through and flake easily. Drain well on kitchen paper. Transfer to a non-metallic bowl and set aside.

3 Heat 250 ml/9 fl oz oil in the same skillet. Add the shallots and fry for about 3 minutes until softened, but not browned. Stir in the carrots, fennel, bay leaves, garlic, chilli flakes, vinegar and salt and pepper to taste.

Bring to the boil, then reduce the heat and simmer for 8 minutes. Stir in the coriander seeds and continue simmering for 2 minutes, or until the carrots are tender.

4 Pour the hot mixture over the monkfish and set aside until completely cool. Cover and chill for at least 24 hours and up to 5 days.

5 Make the batter 30 minutes before you plan to fry. Sift the flour and salt into a large bowl and make a well in the middle. Add the egg yolk and 100 ml/3¹⁄₂ fl oz of the beer and gradually whisk the flour into the liquid to form a thick mixture. Stir in the oil and as much of the remaining beer to make a thick, smooth batter. Cover and let it stand for 30 minutes.

6 Remove the monkfish pieces from the marinade and pat dry on kitchen paper; set aside. Heat enough oil for deep-frying in a large heavy-based saucepan until it sizzles – this takes about 40 seconds. Meanwhile, whisk the egg white until stiff peaks form. Stir the batter, then fold in the egg white.

7 Sift the remaining 4 tablespoons flour onto a plate and season to taste with salt and pepper. Roll the pieces of fish in it, shaking off the excess flour. Dip the monkfish pieces in the batter, then drop in the oil. Work in batches if necessary, to avoid overcrowding the saucepan. Fry for 3–4 minutes until golden. Remove and drain well on kitchen paper. Continue until all the fish is fried, reheating the oil between batches.

8 Serve hot with lemon wedges for squeezing over the fish.

salt cod fritters with spinach
buñelos de bacalao con espinacas

You need to allow 48 hours for soaking the dried salt cod for this dish. If you can't find dried salt cod in the supermarket, try Spanish or Caribbean food shops.

MAKES ABOUT 16

250 g/9 oz dried salt cod in 1 piece

for the batter

140 g/5 oz plain flour

1 tsp baking powder

1/4 tsp salt

1 large egg, beaten lightly

about 150 ml/1/4 pint milk

2 lemon slices

2 fresh parsley sprigs

1 bay leaf

1/2 tbsp garlic–flavoured olive oil

85 g/3 oz baby spinach, rinsed

1/4 tsp smoked sweet, mild or hot Spanish paprika, to taste

olive oil

coarse sea salt, optional

1 quantity Garlic Mayonnaise (see page 232), to serve

1 Place the dried salt cod in a large bowl, cover with cold water and leave to soak for 48 hours, changing the water at least 3 times.

2 Meanwhile, make the batter. Sift the flour, baking powder and salt into a large bowl and make a well. Mix the egg with 100 ml/3 1/2 fl oz of the milk and pour into the well in the flour, stirring to make a smooth

batter with a thick coating consistency. If it seems too thick, gradually stir in the remaining milk; set aside for at least 1 hour.

3 After the salt cod has soaked, transfer it to a large frying pan. Add the lemon slices, parsley sprigs, bay leaf and enough water to cover and bring to the boil. Reduce the heat and simmer for 30–45 minutes until the fish is tender and flakes easily.

4 Meanwhile, prepare the spinach. Heat the oil in a small saucepan over a medium heat. Add the spinach with just its rinsing water clinging to the leaves and cook for 3–4 minutes until wilted.

5 Drain the spinach in a sieve, using the back of a spoon to press out any excess. Finely chop the spinach, then stir it into the batter with the paprika.

6 Remove the fish from the water and flake the flesh into fine pieces, removing all the skin and tiny bones. Stir the flesh into the batter.

7 Heat 5 cm/2 inches of oil in a heavy-based frying pan until it reaches 190°C/375°F or until a day-old cube of bread turns brown in 30 seconds. Use a greased tablespoon or measuring spoon to drop spoonfuls of the batter into the oil and fry for 8–10 minutes until golden brown. Work in batches to avoid crowding the pan. Use a slotted spoon to transfer the fritters to kitchen paper to drain and sprinkle with sea salt, if using.

8 Serve hot or at room temperature with Garlic Mayonnaise for dipping.

grilled sardines 59
sardinas asados

You will find this simple preparation is traditional all along Spain's Mediterranean coast, where the fish are prepared straight off the boats, often grilled over hot coals. Usually these sardines are served simply with lemon wedges for squeezing over the hot fish. Or, serve them with freshly prepared Garlic Mayonnaise (see page 232). An Orange and Fennel Salad (see page 109) complements the sardines for a summer lunch.

For a really robust flavour, insert an anchovy fillet in each fish cavity before grilling.

SERVES 4–6

2 tbsp garlic-flavoured olive oil

12 fresh sardines, deheaded, gutted, backbone removed*

coarse sea salt and pepper

lemon wedges, to serve

1 Preheat the grill to high and brush the grill rack with a little of the garlic-flavoured oil. Brush the sardines with the oil and arrange in a single layer on the grill rack. Sprinkle with salt and pepper to taste.

2 Grill about 10 cm/4 inches from the heat for 3 minutes, or until the skin becomes crisp. Use kitchen tongs to turn the sardines over and brush with more oil and sprinkle with salt and pepper. Continue grilling for 2–3 minutes until the flesh flakes easily and the skin is crisp. Serve at once.

*cook's tips

Look for firm fish with shiny skin and clear, bright eyes. Sardines are best cooked on the day of purchase, and should be refrigerated until they are grilled.

Fishmongers will prepare the sardines, but it is easy to do at home. Working with one sardine at a time, hold it firmly in one hand and snap off the head with your other hand, pulling downwards. This should remove most of the guts with the head, but use a finger to remove any innards that remain. You can then use your thumb and forefinger to grasp the top of the backbone and pull it towards you to remove. Rinse well and pat dry with kitchen paper.

olives wrapped with anchovies
azeitunas envueltos de anchoas

Lively, crowded tapas bars line the narrow, winding streets in San Sebastian in northern Spain, where a vast and varied, appetizing array of fresh tapas is served every day and night into the early hours of the morning. These pinchons *are ideal to nibble while enjoying the draught beer that is popular in the Basque country.*

MAKES 12

12 anchovy fillets in oil, drained
24 pimiento-stuffed green olives in oil, drained

1 Thinly slice each anchovy fillet lengthways. Wrap a half fillet around the middle of each olive, overlapping the ends, and secure with a wooden cocktail stick. Repeat with another olive and anchovy fillet half and slide onto the toothpick. Continue until all the ingredients are used, and you have 12 *pinchons* with 2 anchovy-wrapped olives on each cocktail stick.

variation
Instead of using pimiento-stuffed olives, stuff pitted green or black olives with a blanched anchovy sliver. Proceed with the recipe as above.

Spain's Mediterranean and Atlantic waters offer up a plentiful supply of fish and seafood all year round

prawns wrapped in ham

gambas envueltos en jamón

Only make the dressing for this recipe when tomatoes are at their summer peak and bursting with flavour. Otherwise, serve the cooled prawns with a bowl of Garlic Mayonnaise (see page 232), Romesco Sauce (see page 233) or Mojo Sauce (see page 84) for dipping.

MAKES 16

for the Tomato-Caper Dressing

2 tomatoes, peeled and deseeded*

1 small red onion, chopped very finely

4 tbsp very finely chopped fresh parsley

1 tbsp capers in brine, drained, rinsed and chopped

finely grated rind of 1 large lemon

4 tbsp extra virgin olive oil

1 tbsp sherry vinegar

16 thin slices serrano ham or prosciutto

16 uncooked tiger prawns, peeled and deveined (see page 64), tails left on

extra virgin olive oil

1 First, make the dressing. Finely chop the prepared tomato flesh and put it in a bowl. Add the onion, parsley, capers and lemon rind and gently toss together. Combine the oil and vinegar and add to the other ingredients; set aside until required.

2 Wrap a slice of ham around each prawn and rub with a little of the oil. Place the prawns in a heatproof dish large enough to hold them in a single layer. Bake in a preheated oven, 160°C/325°F/Gas Mark 3, for 10 minutes.

3 Transfer the prawns to a serving platter and spoon the tomato-caper dressing over. Serve at once, or leave to cool to room temperature.

*cook's tip

To peel and deseed tomatoes, remove the stems and cut a small cross in the top of each one. Put the tomatoes into a heatproof bowl, pour over enough boiling water to cover, and leave for 30 seconds. Use a slotted spoon to transfer to a bowl of iced water. Working with 1 tomato at a time, peel off the skin, then cut in half and use a teaspoon to scoop out the cores and seeds.

64 garlic prawns with lemon and parsley
gambas al ajillo con limón y perejil

Although the main ingredients in this simple dish are always the same – prawns, garlic and lemon – it is served in many guises: sometimes the prawns will be unpeeled; sometimes the heads and tails are left on; chillies and parsley are optional ingredients. This dish is best served hot, but the prawns can also be taken out of the oil, left to cool then served chilled.

SERVES 6

60 uncooked large prawns, thawed if using
   frozen

150 ml/¹/₄ pint olive oil

6 garlic cloves, sliced thinly

3 dried hot red chillies, optional

6 tbsp freshly squeezed lemon juice

6 tbsp very finely chopped fresh parsley

French bread, to serve

1 Peel and devein* the prawns and remove the heads, leaving the tails on. Pat the prawns dry.

2 Heat the oil in a large, deep sauté pan or frying pan. Add the garlic and chillies, if using, and stir around until they begin to sizzle. Add the prawns and cook until they turn pink and curl.

3 Use a slotted spoon to transfer the prawns to warm earthenware bowls. Sprinkle each bowl with lemon juice and parsley. Serve at once with plenty of bread to mop up the juices.

*cook's tip
To devein prawns, use a fine-bladed knife to slice along the back from the head end to the tail, then remove the thin, black intestine.

Churches are a prominent feature of the Spanish landscape

peppers stuffed with crab salad

pimientos del piquillo rellenos de ensalada de cangrejo

Most Spanish kitchens contain at least 1 jar or can of sweet pimientos del piquillo, 7.5-cm/3-inch long red peppers that have been roasted, peeled and deseeded, ready for stuffing or slicing to add to stews and salads. Sometimes they are also sold sliced, so make sure you buy the whole ones, preserved in oil or brine, for this recipe.

MAKES 16

for the Crab Salad

240 g/8¹/₂ oz crab meat, drained and squeezed dry

1 red pepper, grilled, peeled (see page 74) and chopped

approx 2 tbsp fresh lemon juice

salt and pepper

200 g/7 oz cream cheese

16 pimientos del piquillo, drained, or freshly roasted peppers,* tops cut off

chopped fresh parsley, to garnish

1 First make the crab salad. Pick over the crab meat and remove any bits of shell. Put half the crab meat in a food processor with the prepared red pepper, 1¹/₂ tablespoons of the lemon juice and seasoning to taste. Process until well blended, then transfer to a bowl. Flake and stir in the cream cheese and remaining crab meat. Taste and add extra lemon juice, if required.

2 Pat dry the *pimientos del piquillo* and scoop out any seeds that remain in the tips. Use a small spoon to divide the crab salad equally between the peppers, stuffing them generously. Arrange on a large serving dish or individual plates, cover and chill until required. Just before serving, sprinkle the stuffed peppers with the chopped parsley.

*cook's tip

If you can't find *pimientos del piquillo*, and have to roast the peppers yourself, use 16 of the long, sweet Mediterranean variety, not bell peppers. If, however, bell peppers are the only ones you can find, cut 4–6 into wedges and spread the crab salad along each wedge.

68

flat bread with vegetables and clams
coca mallorquina

SERVES 4–6

for the dough

400 g/14 oz strong white flour, plus extra for kneading

1 sachet easy-blend dried yeast

1 tsp salt

1/2 tsp sugar

1 tbsp olive oil

1 tbsp dry white wine

225 ml/8 fl oz warm water

2 tbsp extra virgin olive oil

4 large garlic cloves, crushed

2 large onions, sliced thinly

10 pimientos del piquillo (see page 67), drained, patted dry and sliced thinly

250 g/9 oz shelled baby clams in brine (weight in jar), drained and rinsed

salt and pepper

1 To make the dough, stir the flour, yeast, salt and sugar together in a bowl, making a well in the centre. Add the oil and wine to the water, then pour 175 ml/6 fl oz of the liquid into the well. Gradually mix in the flour from the sides, adding the remaining liquid if necessary, until a soft dough forms.

2 Turn out the dough onto a lightly floured surface and knead until smooth. Shape the dough into a ball. Wash the bowl and rub the inside with oil. Return the dough to the bowl and roll it around so that it is lightly coated in oil. Cover the bowl tightly with clingfilm and set aside in a warm place until the dough doubles in volume.

3 Heat the oil in a large, heavy-based frying pan over a medium-high heat. Reduce the heat and add the garlic and onions and fry slowly, stirring frequently, for 25 minutes, or until the onions are golden brown, but not burned.

4 Transfer the onions to a bowl and leave to cool. Add the pepper strips and clams to the bowl and stir together; set aside.

5 Knock back the dough and knead quickly on a lightly floured surface. Cover it with the upturned bowl and leave to stand for about 10 minutes, which will make it easier to roll out.

6 Heavily flour a 32 x 32-cm/12^3/4 x 12^3/4-inch shallow baking tray. Roll out the dough to make a 34-cm/13^1/2-inch square and transfer it to the baking tray, rolling the edges to form a thin rim. Prick the base all over with a fork.

7 Spread the topping evenly over the dough and season with salt and pepper to taste. Bake in a preheated oven, 230°C/450°F/Gas Mark 8, for 25 minutes, or until the rim is golden brown and the onions tips are slightly tinged. Transfer to a wire rack to cool completely. Cut into 12–16 slices.

Overleaf *Sausages and cured hams are among Spain's gastronomic delights*

chickpeas and chorizo 73
garbanzos con chorizo

1 Heat the oil in a large skillet or heavy-based frying pan over a medium heat. Add the onion and garlic and fry, stirring occasionally, until the onion is softened, but not browned. Stir in the chorizo and continue frying until it is heated through.

2 Tip the mixture into a bowl and stir in the chickpeas and peppers. Splash with sherry vinegar and season with salt and pepper to taste. Serve hot or at room temperature, generously sprinkled with parsley, with plenty of crusty bread.

SERVES 4–6

For an authentic touch, present this simple tapas in individual earthenware casseroles called cazuelas, *as it is served throughout Andalusia.*

4 tbsp olive oil

1 onion, chopped finely

1 large garlic clove, crushed

250 g/9 oz chorizo sausage in one piece, casing removed and cut into 1-cm/$\frac{1}{2}$-inch dice

400 g/14 oz canned chickpeas, drained and rinsed

6 pimientos del piquillo (see page 67), drained, patted dry and sliced

1 tbsp sherry vinegar, or to taste

salt and pepper

finely chopped fresh parsley, to garnish

crusty bread slices, to serve

Date palms are one reminder of Spain's Moorish past

74

chorizo & mushroom kebabs
pinchitos de chorizo y champinoñes

These mini kebabs are an example of the type of tapas known as pinchos, *or bite-sized nibbles served on cocktail sticks.* Pinchos *aren't elaborate, but a step up from just putting out a bowl of almonds or olives to enjoy with drinks.*

MAKES 25

2 tbsp olive oil

25 pieces of chorizo sausage, each about 1 cm/¹/₂ inch square (about 100 g/3¹/₂ oz)

25 button mushrooms, wiped and stalks removed

1 green pepper, grilled and peeled,* and cut into 25 squares

1 Heat the oil in a frying pan over a medium-high heat. Add the chorizo and fry for 20 seconds, stirring. Add the mushrooms and continue frying for a further 1–2 minutes until the mushrooms begin to brown and absorb the fat in the frying pan.

2 Thread a green pepper square, a piece of chorizo and a mushroom onto a wooden cocktail stick. Continue until all the ingredients are used. Serve hot or at room temperature.

*cook's tip
To peel peppers, halve lengthways, stem on, which makes removal of the core and seeds simpler. Grill, skin sides up, 5–7.5 cm/2–3 inches from the heat until charred all over. Remove from the heat and place in a plastic bag for 15 minutes, then rub or peel off the skins. Remove any cores and seeds. Alternatively, the peppers can be charred over a flame. Grilled and peeled peppers can be kept for up to 5 days in the fridge, covered with olive oil.

Stopping off for tapas is a daily feature of Spanish life, in the smartest cities or the humblest villages

tiny meatballs with tomato sauce

albondiguitas con salsa de tomates

Meatballs have been a regular feature of Spanish meals for hundreds of years, with the earliest recipes recorded in the thirteenth century. Albondigas, the Spanish word for meatball, comes from the Arabic al-bunduq, meaning hazelnut, presumably a reflection of the round shape. Meatballs are made in various sizes from beef, lamb and pork, and fried or baked. Serve these individually with cocktail sticks for a light tapas* with drinks, or thread 3 meatballs onto a cocktail stick for a more substantial snack, called a racione.

Mojo Sauce (see page 84) and Garlic Mayonnaise (see page 232) are also good with these.

MAKES ABOUT 60

olive oil

1 red onion, chopped very finely

500 g/1 lb 2 oz minced lamb

1 large egg, beaten

2 tsp freshly squeezed lemon juice

$^1/_2$ tsp ground cumin

pinch of cayenne pepper, to taste

2 tbsp very finely chopped fresh mint

salt and pepper

300 ml/$^1/_2$ pint Tomato and Pepper Sauce
(see page 236), to serve

*cook's tip
This is an ideal tapas to serve at a drinks party because the meatballs can be made ahead and both the sauce and meatballs can be served at room temperature. If you freeze the meatballs, allow 3 hours for them to thaw at room temperature.

1 Heat 1 tablespoon of oil in a frying pan over a medium heat. Add the onion and fry for about 5 minutes, stirring occasionally, until soft, but not brown.

2 Remove the frying pan from the heat and set aside to cool. Add the onion to the lamb with the egg, lemon juice, cumin, cayenne, mint and salt and pepper to taste in a large bowl. Use your hands to squeeze all the ingredients together. Fry a small piece of the mixture and taste to see if the seasoning needs adjusting.

3 With wet hands, shape the mixture into about sixty 2-cm/$^3/_4$-inch balls. Place on a tray and chill for at least 20 minutes.

4 When ready to cook, heat a small amount of oil in 1 or 2 large frying pans (the exact amount of oil will depend on how much fat is in the lamb). Arrange the meatballs in a single layer, without overcrowding the frying pan, and fry over a medium-high heat for about 5 minutes until brown on the outside, but still pink inside. Work in batches if necessary, keeping the cooked meatballs warm while you fry the remainder.

5 Gently reheat the Tomato and Pepper Sauce and serve with the meatballs for dipping. These are best served warm with reheated sauce, but they are also enjoyable at room temperature.

chicken livers with sherry glaze
higadillos al jerez

SERVES 4–6

450 g/1 lb chicken livers, thawed if frozen

2 tbsp olive oil

2^1/$_2$ tbsp sherry vinegar

2 tbsp fino sherry

2 shallots, chopped finely

250 ml/9 fl oz chicken stock

1 sprig of fresh thyme

2 tsp clear honey

pinch of cayenne pepper, to taste

salt and pepper

finely chopped fresh parsley, to garnish

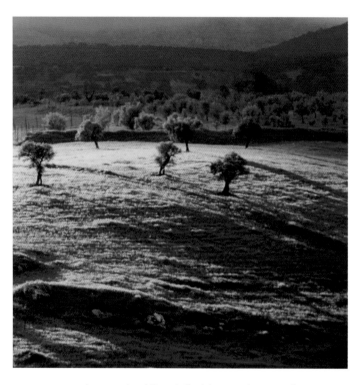

Anyone who visits only Spain's coastal resorts misses out on the huge diversity of the country, geographical and culinary

1 Trim the chicken livers, removing any large veins or green spots; pat dry.

2 Heat the oil in a large frying pan over a medium-high heat. Add the chicken livers in a single layer and cook and stir for about 5 minutes until brown on the outside and just pink inside when you cut one open. Transfer the livers to a heatproof plate and keep warm in a low oven.

3 Add the vinegar, sherry and shallots to the frying pan and bring to the boil, scraping up any crispy bits from the bottom of the frying pan. Add the chicken stock, thyme, honey and cayenne and bubble until reduced to about 4 tablespoons.

4 Return the chicken livers to the frying pan and heat through, stirring to coat with the glaze. Taste and adjust the seasoning and sprinkle with the parsley. Serve at once with wooden cocktail sticks.

broad beans with ham
habas con jamón

SERVES 4–6

225 g/8 oz fresh or frozen shelled broad beans

2 tbsp extra virgin olive oil

1 Spanish red onion, chopped very finely

1 slice medium-thick serrano ham, chopped

fresh parsley, chopped finely, to taste

salt and pepper

French bread, to serve

1 Bring a large saucepan of salted water to the boil. Add the beans and continue to boil for 5–10 minutes until just tender. Drain and put in a bowl of cold water to stop further cooking. Unless the beans are young and tiny, peel off the outer skins.

2 Meanwhile, heat 1 tablespoon of the oil in a frying pan over a medium-high heat. Add the onion and fry for about 5 minutes until soft, but not brown. Add the beans.

3 Stir in the ham and parsley and check the seasoning; the meat is salty, so don't add salt until after tasting. Transfer to a serving bowl and drizzle with the remaining oil. Serve at room temperature with slices of French bread.

The towns of the vast central plains of Spain blend seamlessly with the natural colours of the arid landscape

roasted asparagus with ham
espárragos asados con jamón serrano

In late April, white and green asparagus appears on all menus, often as part of the menú del dia *– the daily special – as Spaniards celebrate the harvest of one of their favourite vegetables. Asparagus is often steamed, but this technique prevents soggy spears, which can happen so quickly.*

To serve as a tapas, arrange the asparagus spears on a platter around a small bowl of sauce so guests can casually dip the spears in the sauce. As a first course, arrange on individual plates with a little sauce spooned over.

SERVES 4–6

sea salt

24 spears fresh asparagus, woody ends snapped off

about 2 tbsp extra virgin olive oil

pepper

12 thin slices serrano ham, halved lengthways

1 x quantity Romesco Sauce (see page 233) or Garlic Mayonnaise (see page 232), to serve

1 Sprinkle a layer of sea salt over the base of a roasting tin that will hold the asparagus spears in a single layer. Brush the asparagus with the olive oil, then lay the spears in the roasting tin.

2 Roast in a preheated oven, 220°C/400°F/Gas Mark 7, for 12–15 minutes until the asparagus is just tender when pierced with the tip of a knife. Remove from the oven and season to taste with freshly ground pepper.

3 As soon as you can hold the spears, wrap a piece of ham around each. Serve hot, warm or at room temperature with a small bowl of Romesco Sauce or Garlic Mayonnaise for dipping.

'wrinkled' potatoes with mojo sauce
papas arraguadas con mojo

Have plenty of chilled beers or water on hand when you serve this classic tapas from the Canary Islands. The potatoes are cooked in heavily salted water to resemble seawater, resulting in a thin film of salt on the skins. The salt and piquant sauce are very thirst-making. If you can't find new red-skinned potatoes, use salad potatoes that hold their shape.

SERVES 4–6

70 g/2^1/$_2$ oz sea salt

24 small, new red-skinned potatoes, unpeeled and
   kept whole

for the Mojo Sauce

40 g/1^1/$_2$ oz day-old bread, crusts removed and torn
   into small pieces

2 large garlic cloves

^{1}/$_2$ tsp salt

1^1/$_2$ tbsp hot Spanish paprika

1 tbsp ground cumin

approx 2 tbsp red wine vinegar

approx 5 tbsp extra virgin olive oil

2 pimientos del piquillo (see page 67), preserved, drained

1 Pour about 2.5 cm/1 inch water in a saucepan and stir in the sea salt. Add the potatoes and stir again: they do not have to be covered with water. Fold a clean tea towel to fit over the potatoes, then bring the water to the boil. Reduce the heat and simmer for 20 minutes, or until the potatoes are tender, but still holding together.

2 Remove the tea towel and set aside. Drain the potatoes and return them to the empty saucepan. When the tea towel is cool enough to handle, wring the saltwater it contains into the saucepan. Put the saucepan over a low heat and shake until the potatoes are dry and coated with a thin white film. Remove from the heat.

3 Meanwhile, make the Mojo Sauce. Put the bread in a bowl and add just enough water to cover; set aside for 5 minutes to soften. Use your hands to squeeze all the water from the bread. Use a pestle and mortar to mash the garlic and salt into a paste. Stir in the paprika and cumin. Transfer the mixture to a food processor. Add 2 tablespoons of vinegar and blend, then add the bread and 2 tablespoons of oil and blend again.

4 With the motor running, add the pepper pieces a few at a time until they are puréed and a sauce forms. Add more oil, if necessary, until the sauce is smooth and thick. Taste and adjust the seasoning, adding extra vinegar, if necessary.

5 To serve, cut the potatoes in half and spear with wooden cocktail sticks. Serve with a bowl of sauce on the side for dipping. The potatoes can be eaten hot or at room temperature.

feisty potatoes
patatas bravas

This classic Catalan tapas is not called 'feisty' for nothing – the sauce should be hot. You will find as many 'authentic' recipes for this dish as there are cooks in Spain. Every cook has their own way: sometimes the potatoes are deep-fried, and often the garlic-flavoured mayonnaise and chilli oil are mixed together. This version is similar to the way they are served at Bar Tomás in the fashionable Barcelona neighbourhood of Sarrià. The bar's patatas bravas *have been voted among the city's best by* La Vanguardia *newspaper.*

SERVES 6
for the Chilli Oil
150 ml/¹/₄ pint olive oil
2 small, hot red chillies, slit
1 tsp hot Spanish paprika

1 x quantity Fried Potatoes (see page 247)
1 x quantity Garlic Mayonnaise (see page 232)

1 To make the chilli oil, heat the oil and chillies over a high heat until the chillies begin to sizzle. Remove from the heat and stir in the paprika. Set aside and leave to cool, then transfer to a pourer with a spout; do not strain.

2 Fry the potatoes, and while they cook make the Garlic Mayonnaise.

3 To serve, divide the potatoes between 6 plates and add a dollop of Garlic Mayonnaise to each. Drizzle with chilli oil and serve warm or at room temperature. In Spain these are served with wooden cocktail sticks.

grilled aubergine dip
salsa de berenjenas

SERVES 6–8

1 large aubergine, about 400 g/14 oz

olive oil

2 spring onions, chopped finely

1 large garlic clove, crushed

2 tbsp finely chopped fresh parsley

salt and pepper

smoked sweet Spanish paprika, to garnish

French bread, to serve

1 Cut the aubergine into thick slices and sprinkle with salt to draw out any bitterness; set aside for 30 minutes, then rinse and pat dry.

2 Heat 4 tablespoons of the oil in a large frying pan over a medium-high heat. Add the aubergine slices and fry on both sides until soft and beginning to brown. Remove from the frying pan and set aside to cool. The slices will release the oil again as they cool.

3 Heat another tablespoon of oil in the frying pan. Add the onions and garlic and fry for 3 minutes until the spring onions become soft. Remove from the heat and set aside with the aubergine slices to cool.

4 Transfer all the ingredients to a food processor and process just until a coarse purée forms. Transfer to a serving bowl and stir in the parsley. Taste and adjust the seasoning, if necessary. Serve at once, or cover and chill until 15 minutes before required. Sprinkle with paprika and serve with slices of French bread.

traditional catalan salt cod salad 89
esqueixada

*In fashionable Barcelona restaurants the salt cod in
this classic salad is served in thin slices with finely
diced tomato, pepper and olives sprinkled round the
plate for the garnish.* This more rustic version,
however, is what you will find in country restaurants.
Similar to ceviche, the fish in this recipe 'cooks' in
the acidity of the vinegar and lemon juice.*

SERVES 4–6

400 g/14 oz dried salt cod in one piece

6 spring onions, sliced thinly on the diagonal

6 tbsp extra virgin olive oil

1 tbsp sherry vinegar

1 tbsp lemon juice

pepper

2 large red peppers, grilled, peeled (see page 74),
    deseeded and diced very finely

12 large black olives, stoned and sliced

2 large, juicy tomatoes, sliced thinly, to serve

2 tbsp very finely chopped fresh parsley, to garnish

1 Place the dried salt cod in a large bowl, cover with
cold water and leave to soak for at least 48 hours,
changing the water occasionally.

2 Pat the salt cod very dry with kitchen paper and
remove the skin and bones, then use your fingers
to tear into fine shreds. Put in a large, non-metallic
bowl with the spring onions, oil, vinegar and lemon
juice and toss together. Season with freshly ground
black pepper, cover and put in the refrigerator to
marinate for 3 hours.

3 Stir in the peppers and olives. Taste and adjust the
seasoning, if necessary, remembering that the cod
and olives might be salty. Arrange the tomato slices on a
large platter or individual plates and spoon the salad on
top. Sprinkle with parsley and serve.

*cook's tip

To prepare the updated version of this salad, put the
desalted salt cod in the freezer for about 30 minutes,
then thinly slice. (If you try to slice the salt cod without
freezing first, the slices will fall apart.)

variations

For a summer tapas, cut vine-ripened cherry tomatoes
in half and use a teaspoon to scoop out the seeds.
Sprinkle with sea salt and turn upside down on kitchen
paper to drain for 30 minutes. Spoon the salad into the
tomato halves and sprinkle with parsley.

The salt cod salad can also be used to stuff *pimientos
del piquillo*, as in the recipe on page 67.

fried cheese
queso frito

The tangy taste of this traditional Spanish sheep's cheese becomes more pronounced when the cheese is heated. These are best served as soon as they are fried, but still enjoyable for up to 30 minutes, but any longer and the cheese becomes rubbery.

MAKES ABOUT 16

200 g/7 oz Manchego cheese, in one piece

55 g/2 oz fresh fine white breadcrumbs

1 tsp dried thyme

1 large egg

olive oil

1 x quantity Romesco Sauce (see page 233),
   to serve (optional)

1 De-rind the cheese, then cut it into 16 wedge-shaped slices, each 0.5–1 cm/^{1}/4–^{1}/2 inch thick; set aside. Mix the breadcrumbs and thyme together on a plate and beat the egg in a soup plate.

2 Dip the cheese wedges, one by one, first in egg, then in breadcrumbs, patting them on all over.

3 Heat 0.5 cm/^{1}/4 inch of oil in a heavy-based frying pan over a medium-high heat until a cube of day-old bread sizzles – this takes about 40 seconds. Add the cheese wedges and fry for about 30 seconds on each side until golden brown and crisp. Work in batches, if necessary, to avoid over-crowding the frying pan.

4 As each wedge is fried, remove it from the frying pan and drain on kitchen paper. Leave to cool slightly, then serve with a bowl of Romesco Sauce for dipping into, if liked.

A monumental column makes an imposing silhouette against the sky at dusk

salads on bread
montaditos

Visit any tapas bar in northern Spain at lunchtime and you'll find plates of bread slices mounded with mayonnaise-based salads that look like two- or three-bite open sandwiches. Ensaladilla Rusa, Russian Salad, diced potatoes, beans, carrots and peas, is a popular, quickly assembled combination, as all Spanish supermarkets sell this prepared mix in jars.

Both of these salads also make a suitable stuffing for pimientos del piquillo (see page 67).

EACH SALAD QUANTITY MAKES 12–14 OPEN SANDWICHES

for the Potato Salad

200 g/7 oz new potatoes, scrubbed and boiled

$^1/_2$ tbsp white wine vinegar

salt and pepper

3–4 tbsp mayonnaise or Garlic Mayonnaise (see page 232)

2 hard-boiled eggs, shelled and chopped finely

2 spring onions, white and green parts chopped finely

12–14 black olives, stoned and sliced, to garnish

for the Tuna Salad

200 g/7 oz canned tuna in olive oil, drained

4 tbsp mayonnaise or Garlic Mayonnaise (see page 232)

2 hard-boiled eggs, shelled and chopped finely

1 tomato, grilled and peeled, deseeded (see page 63) and chopped very finely

2 tsp grated lemon rind, or to taste

cayenne pepper, to taste

salt and pepper

12–14 anchovy fillets in oil, drained, to garnish

24–28 slices from a long, thin loaf, say French bread, cut on a slight diagonal, about 5 mm/$^1/_4$ inch thick

1 To make the potato salad, peel the potatoes as soon as they are cool enough to handle, then cut them into 5-mm/$^1/_4$-inch dice. Toss with the vinegar and season with salt and pepper to taste; set aside to cool completely. Stir in the mayonnaise, then fold in the chopped eggs and spring onions. Taste and adjust the seasoning. Mound generously on the bread slices, then top each with olive slices.

2 To make the tuna salad, flake the drained tuna into a bowl. Stir in the mayonnaise, then fold in the hard-boiled eggs, tomato, lemon rind and cayenne. Taste and adjust the seasoning if necessary. Mound generously on the bread slices, then top each with anchovy fillets.

moorish courgette salad

ensalada de calabacines a la morisco

The combination of toasted pine kernels and plump raisins has featured in Spanish recipes since the Moors ruled the Iberian Peninsula from AD 711 to 1492.

This versatile chilled salad can be spooned onto bread slices as tapas, served as a first course on a bed of lettuce leaves, or as an accompaniment for roast chicken as part of a summer buffet. Make this at least 4 hours in advance, so the flavours blend.

SERVES 4–6

about 4 tbsp olive oil

1 large garlic clove, halved

500 g/18 oz small courgettes, sliced thinly*

55 g/2 oz pine kernels

55 g/2 oz raisins

3 tbsp finely chopped mint leaves (not spearmint or peppermint)

about 2 tbsp lemon juice, or to taste

salt and pepper

1 Heat the oil in a large frying pan over a medium heat. Add the garlic and let it fry until golden to flavour the oil, then remove and discard. Add the courgettes and fry, stirring until just tender. Immediately remove from the frying pan and transfer to a large serving bowl.

2 Add the pine kernels, raisins, mint, lemon juice and salt and pepper to taste, and stir. Taste, and add more oil, lemon juice and seasoning, if necessary.

3 Set aside and leave to cool completely. Cover and chill for at least 3$^1/_2$ hours. Remove from the fridge 10 minutes before serving.

*cook's tip

This salad is best made with young, tender courgettes no more than 2.5 cm/1 inch thick. If using older, larger courgettes, cut them in half or quarters lengthways first, then slice thinly.

variation

For a more robust flavour, chop 4 drained anchovy fillets in oil and add in step 2.

figs with blue cheese
higos con queso picós

A delicious combination of sweet–savoury flavours, and a stylish first course for a dinner party. Cabrales, matured in limestone caves, is Spain's best-known blue cheese, but Picós is a milder version that works well in this recipe. Usually made from sheep's milk, it can, however, contain three types of milk and is traditionally wrapped in vine leaves.

SERVES 6

for the caramelized almonds

100 g/3¹/₂ oz caster sugar

115 g/4 oz whole almonds, blanched or unblanched

12 ripe figs

350 g/12 oz Spanish blue cheese, such as Picós, crumbled

extra virgin olive oil

1 First make the caramelized almonds. Put the sugar in a saucepan over a medium-high heat and stir until the sugar melts and turns golden brown and bubbles: do not stir once the mixture starts to bubble. Remove from the heat and add the almonds one at a time and quickly turn with a fork until coated; if the caramel hardens, return the saucepan to the heat. Transfer each almond to a lightly buttered baking sheet once it is coated. Leave until cool and firm.*

2 To serve, slice the figs in half and arrange 4 halves on each plate. Coarsely chop the almonds by hand. Place a mound of blue cheese on each plate and sprinkle with chopped almonds. Drizzle the figs very lightly with the oil.

variation

Walnut halves can also be caramelized and used in this recipe.

*cook's tip

Store the nuts in an airtight jar for up to 3 days until required; any longer and they become soft.

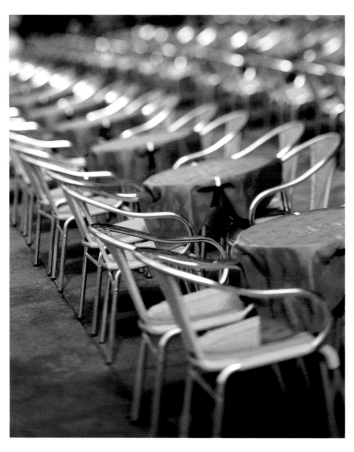

Pavement tables for leisurely lunches are an eye-catching feature of any Spanish city

gazpacho
gazpacho

This is one of the classic chilled soups that is as refreshing as fruit juice on a hot summer's day.

SERVES 4–6

500 g/1 lb 2 oz large, juicy tomatoes, peeled, deseeded (see page 63) and chopped

3 large, ripe red peppers, cored, deseeded and chopped

approx 2 tbsp sherry vinegar

4 tbsp olive oil

pinch of sugar

salt and pepper

to serve

ice cubes

finely diced red pepper

finely diced green pepper

finely diced yellow pepper

finely diced deseeded cucumber

finely chopped hard-boiled eggs

croûtons fried in garlic-flavoured olive oil

1 Put the tomatoes, red peppers, 2 tablespoons of sherry vinegar, the oil and sugar in a food processor and process until blended and as smooth or chunky as you like. Cover and chill for at least 4 hours before serving. Taste and adjust the seasoning, adding extra vinegar if necessary.*

2 To serve, ladle the soup into bowls and add 1 or 2 ice cubes to each. Put a selection of garnishes in bowls and let everyone add their own.

*cook's tip
Cold dulls flavours, so more seasoning will be needed than for a soup served warm. For this reason, taste and adjust the seasoning after chilling the soup.

The heat of the midday sun in much of Spain slows the pace of life, and necessitates refreshing food and drink

roasted tomato soup
sopa de tomates asados

Andalusian and Canary Island farmers grow many of the tomatoes Europeans eat throughout the year. Even in those sunny climates, however, the seemingly never-ending poly-tunnels can produce pale and insipid specimens that benefit from the flavour boost provided by the tomato purée and sherry in this recipe. This richly flavoured soup is best served hot, but it can also be served well chilled. (It is, however, completely different from the uncooked and refreshing Gazpacho on page 99 in both its texture and flavour.)

SERVES 4–6

900 g/2 lb large, juicy tomatoes, halved

2 tbsp butter

1 tbsp olive oil

1 large onion, sliced

2–3 tbsp tomato purée, depending on the flavour of
the tomatoes

900 ml/1 1/2 pints vegetable stock

2 tbsp amontillado sherry

1/2 tsp sugar

salt and pepper

crusty bread, to serve

1 Preheat the grill to high. Place the tomatoes, cut sides up, on a baking sheet and grill about 10 cm/4 inches from the heat for 5 minutes, or until just starting to char on the edges.

2 Meanwhile, melt the butter with the oil in a large saucepan or flameproof casserole over a medium heat. Add the onion and fry for 5 minutes, stirring occasionally. Stir in the tomato purée and continue frying about 2 minutes.

3 Add the tomatoes, stock, sherry, sugar and salt and pepper to taste to the saucepan and stir. Bring to the boil, then reduce the heat to low and simmer, covered, for about 20 minutes until the tomatoes are reduced to a pulp.

4 Process the soup through a mouli* into a large bowl. Return to the rinsed saucepan and reheat, uncovered, simmering 10 minutes, or until the desired consistency is achieved. Ladle into individual bowls and serve with plenty of bread.*

*cook's tips

If you don't possess a mouli, purée the soup in a food processor or blender then work through a fine sieve to achieve the smooth texture.

When serving chilled, swirl 1 tablespoon of soured cream in each bowl and sprinkle with parsley.

102

chilled garlic soup
ajo blanco

SERVES 4–6

500 g/1 lb 2 oz day-old country-style white bread,
   crusts removed and torn

5 large garlic cloves, halved

125 ml/4 fl oz extra virgin olive oil, plus a little extra
   to garnish

4–5 tbsp sherry vinegar, to taste

300 g/10$^{1}/_{2}$ oz ground almonds

1.2 litres/2 pints water, chilled

salt and white pepper

seedless white grapes, to garnish

1 Put the bread in a bowl with just enough cold water
to cover and leave to soak for 15 minutes. Squeeze
the bread dry and transfer it to a food processor.

2 Add the garlic, oil, 4 tablespoons of sherry vinegar
and the ground almonds to the food processor with
250 ml/9 fl oz of the water and process until blended.

3 With the motor running, slowly pour in the
remaining water until a smooth soup forms. Taste
and add extra sherry vinegar if necessary. Cover and
chill for at least 4 hours.

4 To serve, stir well and adjust the seasoning if
necessary. Ladle into bowls and float grapes on top
with a drizzle of olive oil.

*The architecture of old Spain proudly bears the hallmarks
of its Moorish past*

stuffed peppers 105
pimientos rellenos

This is an all-purpose vegetable dish – as well as being served as a tapas, a first course, or a light lunch dish with a sliced tomato salad, these peppers also make a good accompaniment to roast poultry and meat.

MAKES 6

6 tbsp olive oil, plus a little extra for rubbing on peppers

2 onions, chopped finely

2 garlic cloves, crushed

140 g/5 oz Spanish short-grain rice

55 g/2 oz raisins

55 g/2 oz pine kernels

40 g/1^1/$_2$ oz fresh parsley, chopped finely

salt and pepper

1 tbsp tomato purée dissolved in 700 ml/1^1/$_4$ pints hot
    water

4–6 red, green or yellow peppers (or a mix of colours),
    or 6 of the long, Mediterranean variety

1 Heat the oil in a shallow, heavy-based flameproof casserole. Add the onions and fry for about 3 minutes. Add the garlic and fry for a further 2 minutes, or until the onion is soft but not brown.

2 Stir in the rice, raisins and pine kernels until all are coated in the oil, then add half the parsley and salt and pepper to taste. Stir in the dissolved tomato purée and bring to the boil. Reduce the heat and leave to simmer, uncovered, for 20 minutes, shaking the casserole frequently, or until the rice is tender, the liquid is absorbed and small holes appear on the surface: watch carefully because the raisins can catch and burn easily. Stir in the remaining parsley, then set aside and leave to cool slightly.

3 While the rice is simmering, cut the top off each pepper and reserve. Remove the core and seeds from each pepper.*

4 Divide the stuffing equally between the peppers. Use wooden cocktail sticks to secure the tops back in place. Lightly rub each pepper with oil and arrange in a single layer in a baking dish. Bake in a preheated oven, 200°C/400°F/Gas Mark 6, for 30 minutes, or until the peppers are tender. Serve hot or leave to cool to room temperature.

*cook's tip
If you are using the pointed, Mediterranean variety of pepper, a melon baller, teaspoon or small paring knife makes it easier to remove all the seeds.

basque scrambled eggs
piperrada

SERVES 4–6

olive oil

1 large onion, chopped finely

1 large red pepper, cored, deseeded and chopped

1 large green pepper, cored, deseeded and chopped

2 large tomatoes, peeled, deseeded (see page 63)
  and chopped

55 g/2 oz chorizo sausage, sliced thinly, casings
  removed, if preferred

35 g/1¹/₄ oz butter

10 large eggs, beaten lightly

salt and pepper

4–6 thick slices country-style bread, toasted, to serve

1 Heat 2 tablespoons of oil in a large, heavy-based frying pan over a medium-high heat. Add the onion and peppers and cook for about 5 minutes, or until the vegetables are soft, but not brown. Add the tomatoes and heat through. Transfer to a plate and keep warm in a preheated low oven.

2 Add another tablespoon of oil to the frying pan. Add the chorizo and cook for 30 seconds, just to warm through and flavour the oil. Add the sausage to the reserved vegetables.

3 There should be about 2 tablespoons of oil in the frying pan, so add a little extra, if necessary, to make up the amount. Add the butter and allow to melt. Season the eggs with salt and pepper to taste, then add to the frying pan and scramble until cooked to the desired degree of firmness. Return the vegetables to the frying pan and stir through. Serve at once with hot toast.

Few urban dwellings in Spain have gardens, but a balcony is perfect for enjoying the evening atmosphere

orange and fennel salad
ensalada de naranjas y hinojo

SERVES 4

4 large, juicy oranges

1 large fennel bulb, sliced very thinly

1 mild white onion, sliced finely

2 tbsp extra virgin olive oil

12 plump black olives, stoned and sliced thinly

1 red chilli, deseeded and sliced very thinly (optional)

finely chopped fresh parsley

French bread, to serve

1 Finely grate the rind from the oranges into a bowl; set aside. Using a small serrated knife, remove all the white pith from the oranges, working over a bowl to catch the juices. Cut the oranges horizontally into thin slices.

2 Toss the orange slices with the fennel and onion slices. Whisk the oil into the reserved orange juice, then spoon over the oranges. Scatter the olive slices over the top, add the chilli, if using, then sprinkle with the orange rind and parsley. Serve with slices of French bread.

variations

• For a more substantial meal, add soaked and cooked salt cod (see page 56).

• Garnet-red blood oranges look stunning.

• Juicy dark grapes make an interesting alternative to the olives.

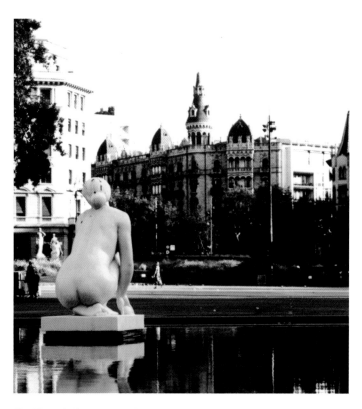

The Plaza de Catalunya in Barcelona is a quieter part of this thronging city

chorizo and quail's eggs
chorizo y huevos de codorniz

1 Preheat the grill to high. Arrange the slices of bread on a baking sheet and grill until golden brown on both sides.

2 Cut or fold the chorizo slices to fit on the toasts; set aside.

3 Heat a thin layer of oil in a large frying pan over a medium heat until a cube of day-old bread sizzles – this takes about 40 seconds. Break the eggs into the frying pan* and fry, spooning the fat over the yolks, until the whites are set and the yolks are cooked to your liking.

4 Remove the fried eggs from the frying pan and drain on kitchen paper. Immediately transfer to the chorizo-topped toasts and dust with paprika. Sprinkle with salt and pepper to taste, and serve at once.

cook's tip
Despite their delicate appearance, quail's eggs can be difficult to crack because of a relatively thick membrane under the shell. It is useful to have a pair of scissors handy to cut through the membrane as you break the eggs into the frying pan.

There isn't anything traditional about this recipe. This is an example of the new style of tapas served in Euro-chic hotel cocktail lounges in Barcelona and Madrid – ideal for enjoying with a chilled flûte of cava.

MAKES 12

12 slices French bread, sliced on the diagonal, about 0.5 cm/^{1}/$_4$ inch thick

about 40 g/1^1/$_2$ oz cured, ready-to-eat chorizo, cut into 12 thin slices

olive oil

12 quail's eggs

mild paprika

salt and pepper

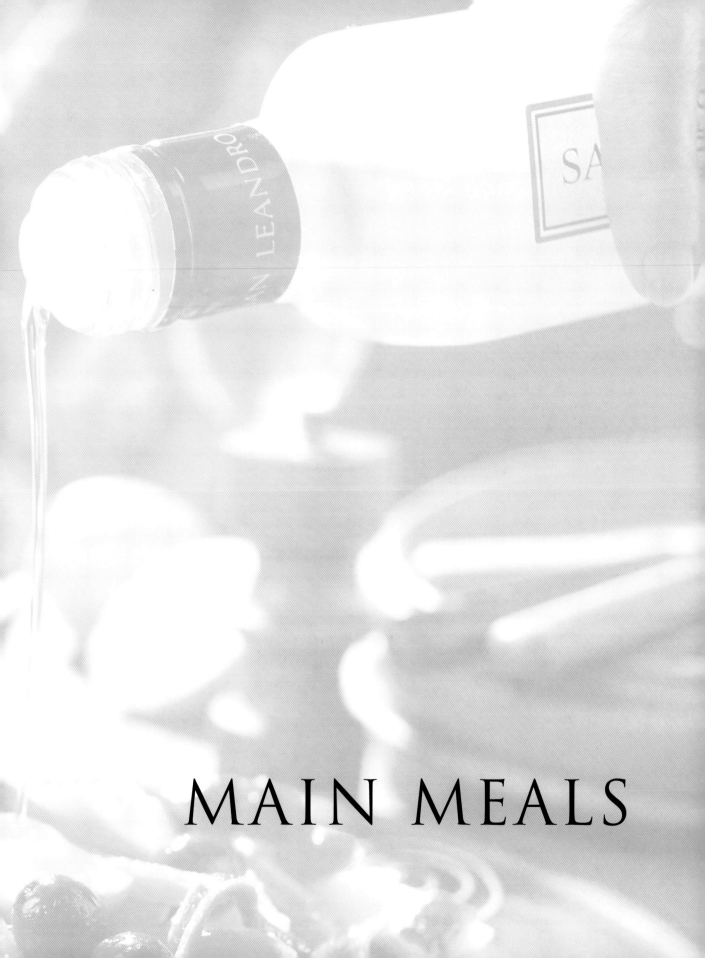

MAIN MEALS

114 Who can think of Spain without conjuring up images of the magnificent seafood dishes offered up by the Mediterranean and the country's other coastal waters? Yet, the Spaniards are great meat-eaters as well, so the choice of main meals is varied. Spanish main courses are served simply and not heavily sauced as they tend to be in neighbouring France.

Spanish cooks usually serve vegetables as an integral part of the main course or as a separate course, rather than on the side, a presentation reflected in dishes such as Chicken Thighs with Broad Beans and Mushrooms (see page 126), Veal with Pickled Vegetables (see page 139), Roasted Garlic-and-rosemary Lamb with Potatoes (see page 143), and Cod with Spinach (see page 169).

Paella (see page 121), the saffron-flavoured rice dish from Valencia, is always popular with Spaniards and tourists alike. The recipe in this chapter includes chicken portions and seafood, but the ingredients can be varied to accommodate whatever you have to hand. Rice and seafood have an affinity, and Black Rice (see page 122), coloured and flavoured by black squid ink, is another Mediterranean favourite.

Restaurants along the Mediterranean specialize in deep-frying almost anything that was swimming the day before, and you can re-create holiday meals at home with Deep-fried Seafood (see page 159).

Yet not all of Spain is hot and sunny all the time, and Pork with Peppers (see page 140) and Lamb Stew with Chickpeas (see page 144) are examples of hearty, richly flavoured Spanish stews that provide warmth during cold winters.

Quails with Grapes (see page 135) is a dish inspired by the Spanish passion for game shooting. It is rich and sweet, and makes an impressive main course for a dinner party.

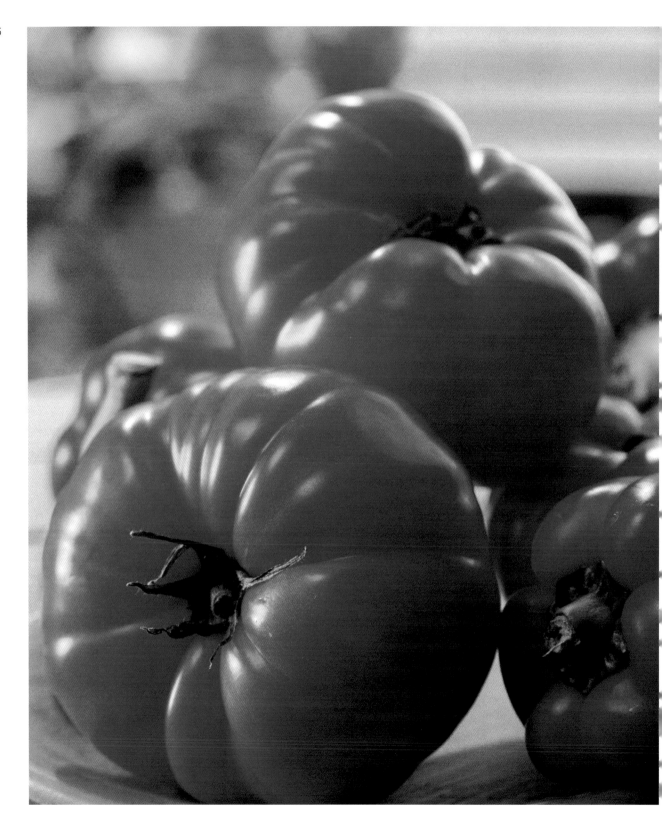

For quick and easy midweek family meals, try Meatballs with Peas (see page 136), Rice with Chorizo and Prawns (see page 125) and Sausages with Lentils (see page 147).

Spanish cuisine scarcely accommodates vegetarians who do not include fish or seafood in their diets. Fortunately, however, egg dishes are always on the menu, and Basque Scrambled Eggs (see page 106) and Eggs on Vegetables (see page 177), minus the chorizo, are both suitable and delicious. Tortilla (see page 42) is another traditional dish that is always available. Fresh salads are of course an option for vegetarians, and the Grilled Pepper Salad (see page 178) from Murcia makes a filling main course served with country-style crusty bread. Although Spanish gardens supply out-of-season vegetables to the rest of Europe, seasonal produce is greatly valued in Spain, so salads are a magnificent feast of vibrant colours and full flavours. During the summer

Seasonal produce is valued in Spain so salads are a magnificent feast of vibrant colours and full flavours

months, as temperatures rise, salads and barbecues become the favoured meals for relaxed eating.

Most main courses will be accompanied by a bottle of wine, although Spaniards are less obsessed with 'rules' such as only white wine with seafood and red wine with meat than, say, the French. More likely, the wine will be whatever is produced locally and it will have a natural affinity with local dishes. However, in the Basque Country and other regions along the Bay of Biscay, a glass of the locally produced cider will be the drink of choice.

Overleaf *The Royal Palace, in Madrid, is spectacular against the skyline*

Unlike risotto, the rice for a good paella is not sticky with sauce, yet each grain should be moist with oil. Stirring disrupts the way the rice cooks. Gradually lowering the heat as the liquid reduces, and giving the paella pan a shake, will help to prevent the rice sticking.

paella
paella

SERVES 6–8

2 pinches of saffron threads

400 g/14 oz Spanish short-grain rice

16 live mussels

about 6 tbsp olive oil

6–8 unboned chicken thighs, excess fat removed, skin on

140 g/5 oz chorizo sausage, cut into 5-mm/^{1}/4-inch slices, casings removed

2 large onions, chopped

4 large garlic cloves, crushed

1 tsp mild or hot Spanish paprika, to taste

100 g/3^1/2 oz French or other green beans, chopped

100 g/3^1/2 oz frozen peas

1.2 litres/2 pints fish, chicken or vegetable stock

salt and pepper

16 uncooked prawns, peeled and deveined (see page 64)

2 sweet red peppers, grilled, peeled (see page 74) and sliced

35 g/1^1/4 oz fresh parsley, chopped finely

1 Put the saffron threads in a small bowl and pour in 4 tablespoons of hot water; set aside. Put the rice in a sieve and rinse until the water runs clear; set aside. Scrub the mussels, removing any beards, and discard any with cracked shells or open ones that do not close when tapped; set aside.

2 Heat 3 tablespoons of oil in a 30-cm/12-inch paella pan or flameproof casserole over a medium-high heat. Add the chicken thighs, skin sides down, and fry for 5 minutes, or until golden and crispy. Transfer to a bowl.

3 Add the chorizo to the paella pan and fry for about 1 minute until it starts to crisp. Add to the chicken.

4 Heat another 3 tablespoons of oil in the paella pan. Add the onions and fry for 2 minutes, then add the garlic and paprika and fry for a further 3 minutes until the onions are soft, but not brown.

5 Add the drained rice, beans and peas to the paella pan and stir until coated in oil. Return the chicken thighs and chorizo and any accumulated juices to the casserole. Stir in the stock, saffron liquid and salt and pepper and bring to the boil, stirring.

6 Reduce the heat to low and simmer, without stirring, for 15 minutes* or until the rice is almost tender and most of the liquid is absorbed.

7 Arrange the mussels, prawns and pepper strips on top, cover the casserole and continue simmering, without stirring, for about 5 minutes until the prawns become pink and the mussels open.

8 Discard any mussels that are not open. Taste and adjust the seasoning. Sprinkle with the parsley and serve at once.

*cook's tip

The first time you make this, preheat the oven to 190°C/375°F/Gas Mark 5 while the paella simmers. Heat sources are not consistent on hobs, so it is hard to say how long it takes for the liquid to be absorbed. If there is too much liquid on the surface, put the dish in the oven, cover and bake for 10 minutes, or until very little liquid remains.

black rice
arroz negro

The easiest way to approach this popular Mediterranean recipe is to buy cleaned squid bodies prepared by a fishmonger. Sachets of squid ink can be bought separately. If, however, you do buy a whole squid, the pearly blue-grey sac containing the ink, which gives the dish its characteristic grey-black colour, is located under the tentacles, and it must be handled gently so it doesn't break.* Use good-quality fish stock, rather than a cube.

SERVES 4–6

400 g/14 oz Spanish short-grain rice

6 tbsp olive oil

1 large onion, sliced finely

2 large garlic cloves, crushed

2 tomatoes, grilled, peeled, deseeded (see page 63), and chopped finely

1 prepared squid body*, cut into 5-mm/$^1/_4$-inch rings (tentacles reserved, if available)

1 litre/1$^3/_4$ pints fish stock

ink sac from squid, or a sachet of squid ink

salt and pepper

12 large raw prawns, shelled and deveined (see page 64)

squid tentacles, if available

2 red peppers, grilled, peeled (see page 74), deseeded and sliced

1 x quantity Garlic Mayonnaise (see page 232), to serve

1 Put the rice in a sieve and rinse until the water runs clear; set aside.

2 Heat the oil in a large, shallow casserole or frying pan over a medium-high heat. Add the onion and fry for 3 minutes, then add the garlic cloves and fry for a further 2 minutes until the onion is soft, but not brown.

3 Add the tomatoes and simmer until they are very soft. Add the squid rings and fry quickly until they turn opaque.

4 Add the rice and stir until it is coated in oil. Pour in the stock, squid ink and salt and pepper to taste and bring to the boil. Reduce the heat and leave to simmer for 15 minutes, uncovered and without stirring, but shaking the frying pan frequently, until most of the stock is absorbed and small holes appear on the surface.

5 Lightly stir in the prawns, squid tentacles, if using, and peppers. Cover the frying pan and continue simmering for about 5 minutes until the prawns turn pink and the tentacles turn opaque and curl.

6 Taste and adjust the seasoning. Serve with Garlic Mayonnaise on the side of each plate.

*cook's tip

To prepare squid, cut off the tentacles just in front of the eyes; discard the hard beak, but reserve the tentacles if they are to be used. Hold the body in one hand and use your other hand to pull out the head, which will bring the innards along as well. Remove and reserve the ink sac, but discard the rest of the innards. Use your fingers to pull out the transparent, quill-like bone in the cavity. Rub off the outer membrane, and cut off and discard the fins. Rinse the squid body and pat dry. You can use the body cavity whole for stuffing, or slice, as for the recipe here.

rice with chorizo and prawns
arroz con chorizo y gambas

The 21st century is well established in Spanish supermarkets, with a seemingly endless array of preserved and prepared ingredients that help make home cooking quick and easy. One example of changing cooking habits is the use of long-grain, quick-cooking rice. If you can't find the Spanish variety, use any quick-cooking rice for this simple midweek supper dish.

SERVES 4

2 tablespoons olive oil

1 large onion, chopped

1 red pepper, cored, deseeded and chopped

1 green pepper, cored, deseeded and chopped

2 large garlic cloves, crushed

1 large tomato, chopped

200 g/7 oz easy-cook Spanish rice

salt and pepper

200 g/7 oz chorizo sausage, cut into 5-mm/^{1}/$_4$-inch
  slices, casings removed

450 ml/16 fl oz vegetable, fish or chicken stock

450 g/1 lb large uncooked prawns, peeled and deveined
  (see page 64)

2 tbsp finely chopped fresh parsley, to garnish

1 Heat the oil in a large, lidded frying pan over a medium-high heat. Add the onion and peppers and fry for 2 minutes. Add the garlic and continue frying, stirring occasionally, for 3 minutes, or until the onion and peppers are soft, but not brown.

2 Add the tomato, rice and salt and pepper to taste and continue cooking for 2 minutes.

3 Stir in the chorizo, then the stock and bring to the boil. Reduce the heat to low, cover and simmer for about 15 minutes until the rice is tender, but still moist.

4 Stir in the prawns, cover and cook for about 5 minutes until they turn pink and the liquid has been absorbed: if the rice remains too moist, simmer for a further 2 minutes, uncovered. Taste and adjust the seasoning if necessary. Sprinkle with parsley and serve.

chicken thighs with broad beans and mushrooms
muslos de pollo con habas y champiñones

Many people have been put off broad beans by the thought of their unappetizing and tough grey skins. Unless the beans are young and tiny, it is best to blanch them before cooking.

SERVES 4

300 g/10¹/₂ oz fresh or frozen shelled broad beans

olive oil

8 unboned chicken thighs, excess fat removed, skin on

1 large onion, sliced finely

1 large garlic clove, crushed

500 g/1 lb 2 oz chestnut mushrooms, wiped and
   sliced thickly

salt and pepper

500 ml/18 fl oz chicken stock

finely chopped fresh parsley, to garnish

Fried Potatoes (see page 247), to serve

1 To blanch the beans, bring a large saucepan of salted water to the boil, add the beans and continue boiling for 5–10 minutes until just tender. Drain and put in a bowl of cold water to stop further cooking. Peel off the outer skins; set aside.

2 Heat 2 tablespoons of the oil in a large, lidded frying pan or flameproof casserole over a medium-high heat. Add 4 chicken thighs, skin sides down, and fry for 5 minutes, or until the skins are crisp and golden. Remove from the frying pan and keep warm and fry the remaining thighs, adding a little extra oil if necessary.

3 Drain off all but 2 tablespoons of the fat in the frying pan. Add the onion and fry for 3 minutes, then add the garlic and continue frying for 5 minutes until the onion is golden. Stir in the mushrooms and salt and pepper to taste and continue frying for 2 minutes, or until the mushrooms absorb all the fat and begin to give off their juices.

4 Return the chicken thighs to the frying pan, skin sides up. Pour in the chicken stock and bring to the boil. Reduce the heat to low, cover tightly and simmer for 15 minutes.

5 Add the beans and continue simmering for 5 minutes until the beans are tender* and the chicken juices run clear when a thigh is pierced. Taste and adjust the seasoning. Sprinkle with parsley and serve with Fried Potatoes.

*cook's tip
Unblanched broad beans can take up to 20 minutes to cook, depending on their age. Frozen beans can be added straight from the freezer in Step 5 and simmered for 5 minutes until tender.

chicken with garlic

pollo ajo

You'll find versions of this simple dish at country restaurants all over Spain. The slow, gentle cooking of the garlic removes the pungency and makes it meltingly tender – mash it on the side of your plate to spread on the chicken pieces. Serve this with Fried Potatoes (see page 247).

SERVES 4–6

4 tbsp plain flour

Spanish paprika, either hot or smoked sweet, to taste

salt and pepper

1 large chicken, about 1.75 kg/3³/4 lb, cut into 8 pieces, rinsed and patted dry

4–6 tbsp olive oil

24 large garlic cloves, peeled and halved

450 ml/³/4 pint chicken stock, preferably home-made

4 tbsp dry white wine, such as white Rioja

2 sprigs fresh parsley, 1 bay leaf and 1 sprig fresh thyme, tied together

fresh parsley and thyme leaves, to garnish

1 Sift the flour onto a large plate and season with paprika and salt and pepper to taste. Dredge the chicken pieces with the flour on both sides, shaking off the excess.

2 Heat 4 tablespoons of the oil in a large, deep frying pan or flameproof casserole over a medium heat. Add the garlic pieces and fry, stirring frequently, for about 2 minutes to flavour the oil. Remove with a slotted spoon and set aside to drain on kitchen paper.

3 Add as many chicken pieces, skin-side down, as will fit in a single layer. (Work in batches if necessary, to avoid over-crowding the frying pan, adding a little extra oil if necessary.) Fry for 5 minutes until the skin is golden brown. Turn over and fry for 5 minutes longer.

4 Pour off any excess oil. Return the garlic and chicken pieces to the frying pan and add the chicken stock, wine and herbs. Bring to the boil, then reduce the heat, cover and simmer for 20–25 minutes until the chicken is cooked through and tender and the garlic very soft.

5 Transfer the chicken pieces to a serving platter and keep warm. Bring the cooking liquid to the boil, with the garlic and herbs, and boil until reduced to about 300 ml/¹/2 pint. Remove and discard the herbs. Taste and adjust the seasoning, if necessary.

6 Spoon the sauce and the garlic cloves over the chicken pieces. Garnish with the parsley and thyme, and serve.

paprika chicken on a bed of onions and ham
pollo al pimentón sobre cebollas y jamón

Marinating chicken breasts in lemon juice is an old trick for tenderizing the flesh. For best results, leave the chicken in the marinade overnight.

SERVES 4

4 chicken breast fillets, skin on

150 ml/^{1}/4 pint freshly squeezed lemon juice

1–1^1/2 tsp mild or hot Spanish paprika, to taste

salt and pepper

about 2 tbsp olive oil

70 g/2^1/2 oz serrano ham, diced

4 large onions, sliced thinly

125 ml/4 fl oz dry white wine

125 ml/4 fl oz chicken stock

fresh thyme or chopped fresh parsley, to garnish

The normally busy streets of Spanish towns may seem abandoned during the siesta

1 To marinate the chicken, put the breasts in a non-metallic bowl. Pour over the lemon juice and leave to marinate in the fridge overnight.

2 When you are ready to cook, remove the chicken breasts from the marinade and pat dry. Rub the skins with the paprika and salt and pepper to taste.

3 Heat 2 tablespoons of the oil in a large, lidded heavy-based frying pan or flameproof casserole over a medium-high heat. Add the chicken breasts, skin-sides down, and fry for 5 minutes, or until the skins are crisp and golden; remove from the frying pan.

4 Stir the ham into the fat remaining in the frying pan, cover and cook for about 2 minutes until it renders any more fat. Add the onions and continue frying, stirring occasionally and adding a little extra oil if necessary, for about 5 minutes until they are soft, but not brown.

5 Add the wine and stock and bring to the boil, stirring. Return the chicken breasts to the frying pan and season with salt and pepper to taste. Reduce the heat, cover and simmer for 20 minutes, or until the chicken is cooked through and the juices run clear.

6 Transfer the chicken to a plate and keep warm in a preheated oven. Bring the sauce to the boil and bubble until the juices reduce. Taste and adjust the seasoning. Divide the onion mixture between 4 warmed plates and arrange a chicken breast on top of each. Garnish with the herbs and serve at once.

132 duck legs with olives
muslos de pato con azeitunas

Duck features in recipes from Navarre, Catalonia and Andalusia. This one is very simple to prepare.

SERVES 4

4 duck legs, all visible fat trimmed off

800 g/1 lb 12 oz canned tomatoes, chopped

8 garlic cloves, peeled, but left whole

1 large onion, chopped

1 carrot, peeled and chopped finely

1 celery stick, peeled and chopped finely

3 sprigs fresh thyme

100 g/3^1/$_2$ oz Spanish green olives stuffed with pimientos
   in brine, rinsed

salt and pepper

1 tsp finely grated orange rind

Colourful architectural features are set off beautifully by an equally vivid sky

1 Put the duck legs in the bottom of a flameproof casserole or a large, heavy-based frying pan with a tight-fitting lid. Add the tomatoes, garlic, onion, carrot, celery, thyme and olives and stir together. Season with salt and pepper to taste.

2 Turn the heat to high and cook, uncovered, until the ingredients begin to bubble. Reduce the heat to low, cover tightly and simmer for 1^1/$_4$–1^1/$_2$ hours until the duck is very tender. Check occasionally and add a little water if the mixture appears to be drying out.

3 When the duck is tender, transfer it to a serving platter, cover and keep hot in a preheated warm oven. Leave the casserole uncovered, increase the heat to medium and cook, stirring, for about 10 minutes until the mixture forms a sauce. Stir in the orange rind, then taste and adjust the seasoning if necessary.

4 Mash the tender garlic cloves with a fork and spread over the duck legs. Spoon the sauce over the top. Serve at once.

quails with grapes
codornices con uvas

Shooting is a popular pastime in Spain, and a wide variety of game dishes appear on many restaurant menus.

SERVES 4

for the Potato Pancake

600 g/1 lb 5 oz unpeeled potatoes

35 g/1¼ oz unsalted butter or pork fat

1½ tbsp olive oil

4 tbsp olive oil

8 quails, gutted

280 g/10 oz green seedless grapes

225 ml/8 fl oz grape juice

2 cloves

about 150 ml/¼ pint water

salt and pepper

2 tbsp Spanish brandy

1 First, par-boil the potatoes for the pancake for 10 minutes. Drain and leave to cool completely, then peel, coarsely grate and season with salt and pepper to taste; set aside.

2 Heat the oil in a heavy-based frying pan or flameproof casserole large enough to hold the quail in a single layer over a medium heat. Add the quail and fry on all sides until they are golden brown.

3 Add the grapes, grape juice, cloves, enough water to come halfway up the side of the quails and salt and pepper to taste. Cover and simmer for 20 minutes. Transfer the quails and all the juices to a roasting tin, unless cooking in a casserole, and sprinkle with brandy. Place in a preheated oven, 230°C/450°F/Gas Mark 8, and roast, uncovered, for 10 minutes.

4 Meanwhile, to make the potato pancake, melt the butter or fat with the oil in a 30-cm/12-inch non-stick frying pan over a high heat. When the fat is hot, add the potato and spread into an even layer. Reduce the heat and simmer for 10 minutes. Place a plate over the frying pan and, wearing oven gloves, invert them so the potato pancake drops onto the plate. Slide the potato back into the frying pan and continue cooking for 10 minutes, or until cooked through and crisp. Slide out of the frying pan and cut into 4 wedges, and keep warm until the quail is ready.

5 Place a potato pancake wedge and 2 quails on each plate. Taste the grape sauce and adjust the seasoning if necessary. Spoon over the quails and serve.

meatballs with peas
albondigas con guisantes

SERVES 4–6

500 g/1 lb 2 oz lean minced beef

1 onion, grated

55 g/2 oz fresh white breadcrumbs

1 egg, beaten lightly

25 g/1 oz fresh parsley, chopped finely

salt and pepper

olive oil

2 large onions, sliced thinly

1 quantity Tomato and Pepper Sauce (see page 236)

200 g/7 oz frozen peas

1 Put the meat in a bowl with the grated onion, breadcrumbs, egg, parsley and salt and pepper to taste. Use your hands to squeeze all the ingredients together. Fry a small piece of the mixture and taste to see if the seasoning needs adjusting.

2 With wet hands, shape the mixture into 12 balls. Put on a plate and chill for at least 20 minutes.

3 When ready to cook, heat a small amount of the oil in 1 or 2 large frying pans: the exact amount needed will depend on how much fat there is in the beef. Arrange the meatballs in a single layer, without over-crowding, and fry, stirring, for about 5 minutes until brown on the outside; work in batches if necessary.

4 Set the meatballs aside and remove all but 2 tablespoons of oil from the frying pan. Add the sliced onions and fry for about 5 minutes until soft, but not brown. Return the meatballs to the frying pan.

5 Stir the Tomato and Pepper Sauce into the frying pan and bring to the boil, gently spooning the sauce and onions over the meatballs. Reduce the heat, cover and simmer for 20 minutes. Add the peas and continue simmering for 7–10 minutes until the peas are tender and the meatballs cooked through. Serve at once.

veal with pickled vegetables
ternera con verduras en escabeche

1 To make the vegetable *escabeche*, heat the oil in a frying pan over a medium heat. Add the shallots and saffron and fry for 5–7 minutes until the shallots begin to caramelize. Add the carrots, beans and cauliflower. Reduce the heat to very low, cover and cook for 5–8 minutes until the vegetables are tender-crisp. Stir in the vinegar, coriander seeds, peppercorns and bay leaf. Remove from the heat and leave to cool, unless you are serving the dish immediately.

The escabeche mixture can be made up to two days in advance and stored in olive oil in a covered container in a refrigerator, and then reheated as the veal chops grill. It also goes well with grilled steaks or pork chops or roasted poultry.

2 When ready to cook, lightly drizzle the chops with more oil and season with salt and pepper to taste. Place under a preheated hot grill, about 10 cm/4 inches from the source of the heat, and grill for 3 minutes. Turn the chops over and grill for a further 2 minutes if you like them cooked medium.

SERVES 4

for the vegetable escabeche

150 ml/¹/4 pint olive oil

4 shallots, sliced

2 pinches of saffron threads

450 g/1 lb young carrots, peeled and sliced thinly

225 g/8 oz French or other green beans, chopped small

225 g/8 oz tiny cauliflower florets

3 tbsp white wine vinegar

1 tsp coriander seeds, crushed

¹/2 tsp black peppercorns, crushed

1 bay leaf, torn in half

3 Transfer the chops to individual plates and spoon a little of the *escabeche* on the side of each. Sprinkle the vegetables with the chives, and drizzle with a little of the flavoured oil. Serve at once.

4 veal loin chops, about 225 g/8 oz each and
   2 cm/³/4 inch thick

salt and pepper

2 tbsp finely snipped fresh chives, to garnish

garlic-flavoured olive oil, for drizzling

Spanish cities are richly endowed with palaces and monuments, sources of civic pride

pork with peppers
espalda de cerdo al chilindrón

Cooking al chilindrón *is popular throughout Spain, but it was originally from the northern regions of Navarre and Aragon, where the rugged conditions demanded hearty, full-flavoured dishes. The dried chillies in this recipe provide a close-to-authentic fiery flavour, so for a milder dish, use dried* ñora *chillies. You need to marinate the pork for at least 8 hours, preferably overnight.*

SERVES 4–6

900 g/2 lb pork shoulder, boned and trimmed, but left in
  1 piece

225 ml/8 fl oz dry white wine

6 garlic cloves, crushed

2 dried ancho or pasila chillies

about 4 tbsp olive oil

2 large onions, chopped

4 red or green peppers, or a mixture, grilled, peeled
  (see page 74), deseeded and sliced

$^1/_2$ tsp hot paprika

800 g/1 lb 12 oz canned chopped tomatoes

2 sprigs fresh thyme

2 sprigs fresh parsley

salt and pepper

1 Place the pork in a non-metallic bowl. Pour over the wine and add 4 of the garlic cloves. Cover with clingfilm and leave to marinate in the fridge for at least 8 hours.

2 Put the chillies in a heatproof bowl and pour over enough boiling water to cover. Leave for 20 minutes to soften, then deseed and chop; set aside.

3 Heat 4 tablespoons of oil in a large, heavy-based flameproof casserole over a medium-high heat. Add the onions and fry for 3 minutes, then add the remaining garlic cloves, chopped chilli, pepper slices and paprika, and fry for a further 2 minutes until the onions are soft, but not brown. Use a slotted spoon to transfer the mixture to a plate, leaving as much oil as possible in the casserole.

4 Drain the pork, reserving the marinade, and pat dry. Add the pork to the casserole, and fry until brown on both sides.

5 Return the onion mixture to the casserole with the pork and stir in the reserved marinade, tomatoes with their juices, the herbs and salt and pepper to taste. Bring to the boil, scraping any glazed bits from the base of the pan. Transfer the casserole to a preheated oven, 160°C/325°F/Gas Mark 3, and cook for 1 hour, or until the pork is tender.

6 If the juices are too thin, remove the pork from the casserole and keep warm. Put the casserole over a high heat and let the juices bubble until reduced to the desired consistency.

7 Taste and adjust the seasoning. Cut the pork into serving pieces and serve with the peppers and sauce from the casserole.

roasted garlic-and-rosemary lamb with potatoes 143
cordero asado con ajo y romero

Wonderful aromas will fill the kitchen while this simple recipe from Aragon roasts. The northern region is known for its suckling lamb, with the tender flesh flavoured by the animal grazing on wild herbs. For the full garlic flavour, the lamb needs to marinate for at least 2 hours.

SERVES 6–8

15 garlic cloves, unpeeled, but separated into cloves

olive oil

1 leg of lamb, about 1.3 kg/3 lb

handful of fresh, tender rosemary sprigs

salt and pepper

24 new potatoes, scrubbed, but left whole

250 ml/9 fl oz full-bodied red wine, say one from Rioja or Navarre

1 Rub the garlic cloves with a little oil in your hands so they are coated. Place them in a small roasting tin and roast in a preheated oven, 200°C/400°F/Gas Mark 6, for 20 minutes, or until very soft; cover the garlic with foil, shiny side in, if the cloves begin to brown too much.

2 As soon as the garlic is cool enough to handle, peel the cloves. Use the back of a fork, or a pestle and mortar, to pound the garlic into a coarse paste with 1/2 teaspoon of oil. Make small incisions all over the lamb, then rub in the garlic paste. Leave to marinate for at least 2 hours in a cool place.

3 When you are ready to cook, place the lamb in a roasting tin on a bed of rosemary sprigs, and season with salt and pepper. Rub the potatoes with oil and place around the lamb. Sprinkle with more rosemary and season with salt and pepper to taste. Roast in a preheated oven, 230°C/450°F/Gas Mark 8, for 10 minutes, then lower the heat to 180°C/350°F/Gas Mark 4 for 15 minutes per 500 g/1 lb 2 oz plus an extra 15 minutes for medium, or until the temperature reaches 70°C/160°F on an internal meat thermometer.

4 Transfer the lamb to a carving plate and leave to stand for 10 minutes before carving. The potatoes should be tender at this point, but if not, return them to oven in a separate dish while you deglaze the tin.

5 Reserve the rosemary sprigs and skim off any fat in the tin. Pour the wine into the tin and bring to the boil, scraping up any glazed bits from the base. Continue boiling until reduced to half. Taste and adjust the seasoning.

6 Slice the lamb and serve with the potatoes and juices spooned round.

144 lamb stew with chickpeas
caldereta de cordero con garbanzos

SERVES 4–6

olive oil

225 g/8 oz chorizo sausage, cut into 5-mm/1/4-inch
   thick slices, casings removed

2 large onions, chopped

6 large garlic cloves, crushed

900 g/2 lb boned leg of lamb, cut into 5-cm/2-inch
   chunks

250 ml/9 fl oz lamb stock or water

125 ml/4 fl oz red wine, such as Rioja or Tempranillo

2 tbsp sherry vinegar

800 g/1 lb 12 oz canned chopped tomatoes

salt and pepper

4 sprigs fresh thyme

2 bay leaves

1/2 tsp sweet Spanish paprika

800 g/1 lb 12 oz canned chickpeas, rinsed and drained

sprigs fresh thyme, to garnish

1 Heat 4 tablespoons of oil in a large, heavy-based flameproof casserole over a medium-high heat. Reduce the heat, add the chorizo and fry for 1 minute; set aside. Add the onions to the casserole and fry for 2 minutes, then add the garlic and continue frying for 3 minutes, or until the onions are soft, but not brown. Remove from the casserole and set aside.

2 Heat a further 2 tablespoons of oil in the casserole. Add the lamb cubes in a single layer without over-crowding the casserole, and fry until browned on each side; work in batches, if necessary.

3 Return the onion mixture to the casserole with all the lamb. Stir in the stock, wine, vinegar, tomatoes with their juices and salt and pepper to taste. Bring to the boil, scraping any glazed bits from the base of the casserole. Reduce the heat and stir in the thyme, bay leaves and paprika.

4 Transfer to a preheated oven, 160°C/325°F/Gas Mark 3, and cook, covered, for 40–45 minutes until the lamb is tender. Stir in the chickpeas and return to the oven, uncovered, for 10 minutes,* or until they are heated through and the juices are reduced.

5 Taste and adjust the seasoning. Garnish with thyme and serve.

cook's tip
If the juices seem too thin, put the casserole on the hob and use a slotted spoon to remove the meat and chickpeas; keep warm. Bring the juices to the boil and boil until reduced; then return the other ingredients.

Although Algerian in origin, spicy merguez *sausages* have made their way into Spanish markets, and are ideal in this hearty pepper and lentil dish. Chorizo, cut into 4-cm/1¹/₂-inch cubes, is also suitable, as are other fresh pork, wild boar or beef sausages.

sausages with lentils 147
salchichas merguez con lentejas

SERVES 4–6

2 tbsp olive oil

12 merguez sausages

2 onions, chopped finely

2 red peppers, cored, deseeded and chopped

1 orange or yellow pepper, cored, deseeded and chopped

280 g/10 oz small green lentils, rinsed

1 tsp dried thyme or marjoram

450 ml/16 fl oz vegetable stock

salt and pepper

4 tbsp chopped fresh parsley

red wine vinegar, to serve

1 Heat the oil in a large, preferably non-stick, lidded frying pan over a medium-high heat. Add the sausages and cook, stirring frequently, for about 10 minutes until they are brown all over and cooked through; remove from the frying pan and set aside.

2 Pour off all but 2 tablespoons of oil from the frying pan. Add the onions and peppers and cook for about 5 minutes until soft, but not brown. Add the lentils and thyme or marjoram and stir until coated with oil.

3 Stir in the stock and bring to the boil. Reduce the heat, cover and simmer for about 30 minutes until the lentils are tender and the liquid is absorbed; if the lentils are tender, but too much liquid remains, uncover the frying pan and simmer until it evaporates. Season to taste with salt and pepper.

4 Return the sausages to the frying pan and reheat. Stir in the parsley. Serve the sausages with lentils on the side, then splash a little red wine vinegar over each portion.

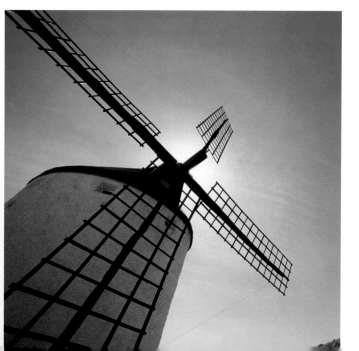

Left *The windswept landscape of La Mancha provides excellent growing conditions for saffron, olives and grapes*

Overleaf *The cook in Spain has a splendid choice of freshly landed fish and seafood*

150

roast monkfish with romesco sauce
rape asado con romesco

Serve this with Saffron Rice with Green Vegetables (see page 244) or Fried Potatoes (see page 247).

SERVES 4–6
900 g/2 lb monkfish in 1 piece
2–3 slices serrano ham
olive oil
salt and pepper
1 x quantity Romesco Sauce (see page 233), to serve

1 Remove the thin membrane covering the monkfish, then rinse the tail and pat it dry. Wrap the ham around the monkfish and rub lightly with oil. Season with salt and pepper. Put on a baking sheet.

2 Roast the monkfish in a preheated oven, 200°C/400°F/Gas Mark 6, for 20 minutes until the flesh is opaque and flakes easily: test by lifting off the ham along the central bone and cut a small amount of the flesh away from the bone to see if it flakes.

3 Cut through the ham to remove the central bone and produce 2 thick fillets. Cut each fillet into 2 or 3 pieces and arrange on a plate with a dollop of Romesco Sauce. Serve at once.

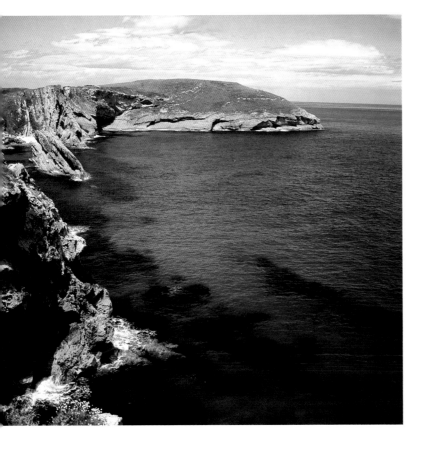

Spain has rich fishing grounds off both its Atlantic and Mediterranean coasts

spaghetti with prawns
espaguetis con gambas

If only Italy comes to mind when you think of seafood pasta dishes, think again. Pasta and pizzas are popular in small, inexpensive restaurants throughout Spain, too. At the beach resort of La Manga, south of Alicante, dishes such as this one feature on many menus.

SERVES 4

450 g/1 lb dried spaghetti

125 ml/4 fl oz olive oil

6 garlic cloves, sliced thinly

450 g/1 lb medium uncooked prawns, peeled
   and deveined (see page 64)

30 g/1 oz flat-leaved parsley, chopped finely,
   plus 2 tbsp extra for garnishing

125 ml/4 fl oz dry white wine

4 tbsp freshly squeezed lemon juice

salt and pepper

1 Bring a large saucepan of salted water to boil over a high heat. Add the spaghetti, return the water to the boil and continue boiling for 10 minutes (check the packet instructions), or until tender.

2 Meanwhile, heat the oil in another large saucepan over a medium heat. Add the garlic and fry until just golden brown. Add the prawns and 30 g/1 oz chopped parsley and stir. Add the wine and simmer for 2 minutes. Stir in the lemon juice and continue simmering until the prawns turn pink and curl.

3 Drain the spaghetti. Tip into the saucepan with the prawns and toss. Add salt and pepper to taste.

4 Transfer to a large serving platter and sprinkle with the extra parsley. Serve at once.

*Gaudi's cathedral, Sagrada Familia,
in Barcelona*

mussels with fennel
mejillónes con hinojo

SERVES 4–6

4 tbsp olive oil

2 large onions, sliced thinly

1 fennel bulb, trimmed and sliced thinly

2 large garlic cloves, chopped finely

350 ml/12 fl oz dry white wine, say a
    white Rioja

100 ml/3 1/2 fl oz fino sherry

400 g/14 oz canned tomatoes

pinch of sugar

salt and pepper

2 kg/4 lb 8 oz live mussels

handful finely chopped fresh parsley

1 Heat the oil in a large, heavy-based saucepan or stockpot over a medium-high heat. Add the onions and fennel and fry for 3 minutes, stirring. Add the garlic and fry for a further 2 minutes, or until the onions and fennel are soft, but not brown.

2 Add the wine and sherry and let them bubble until reduced by half. Add the tomatoes with their juices and bring to the boil, stirring. Add the sugar and salt and pepper to taste, reduce the heat and simmer for 5 minutes, uncovered.

3 Meanwhile, prepare the mussels. Cut off and discard any beards, then scrub any dirty shells. Discard any mussels with broken shells or open ones that do not close when tapped.

4 Reduce the heat under the saucepan to very low. Add the mussels, cover and simmer, shaking the saucepan frequently, for 4 minutes. Discard any mussels that have not opened; remove the remainder and divide them between 4 serving bowls. Re-cover the saucepan and continue simmering for a further minute.

5 Stir the parsley into the juices in the saucepan. Taste and adjust the seasoning. Pour the juices over the bowls of mussels, and serve at once with plenty of bread for mopping up the juices.

156 catalan fish stew
zarzuela

1 Put the saffron threads in a heatproof bowl, add 4 tablespoons of boiling water; set aside to infuse.

2 Heat the oil in a large, heavy-based flameproof casserole over a medium-high heat. Reduce the heat to low, add the onion and fry for 10 minutes, or until golden, but not brown. Stir in the garlic, thyme, bay leaves and red peppers and continue frying for a further 5 minutes, or until the peppers are soft and the onions have softened further.

3 Add the tomatoes and paprika and continue to simmer for 5 minutes, stirring frequently.

4 Stir in the fish stock, reserved saffron water and ground almonds and bring to the boil, stirring frequently. Reduce the heat and simmer for 5–10 minutes until the sauce reduces and thickens. Add salt and pepper to taste.

5 Meanwhile, prepare the mussels and clams. Cut off and discard any beards from the mussels, then scrub any dirty shells.

6 Gently stir in the hake so it doesn't break up and add the prawns, mussels and clams. Reduce the heat to very low, cover the casserole and simmer for about 5 minutes until the hake is cooked through, the prawns turn pink and the mussels and clams open; discard any mussels or clams that remain closed. Serve at once with plenty of thick, crusty bread for soaking up the juices.

This traditional recipe takes its name from the Spanish word meaning 'variety show', which reflects the variety of seafood you will find in the stew. Although the fish and shellfish will vary with the day's catch, saffron, almonds, garlic and tomatoes typically feature.

SERVES 4–6

large pinch of saffron threads

6 tbsp olive oil

1 large onion, chopped

2 garlic cloves, chopped finely

$1^1/_2$ tbsp chopped fresh thyme leaves

2 bay leaves

2 red peppers, cored, deseeded and chopped coarsely

800 g/1 lb 12 oz canned chopped tomatoes

1 tsp sweet smoked paprika

250 ml/9 fl oz fish stock

140 g/5 oz blanched almonds, toasted (see page 50) and ground finely

salt and pepper

12–16 live mussels with uncracked, tightly closed shells (discard any open ones that do not close when tapped)

12–16 live clams with uncracked, tightly closed shells (discard any open ones that do not close when tapped)

600 g/1 lb 5 oz thick, boned hake or cod* fillets, skinned and cut into 5-cm/2-inch chunks

12–16 uncooked prawns, heads and tails removed and deveined (see page 64)

thick, crusty bread, to serve

*cook's tips

Take care not to overcook the hake or it will break into flakes that have very little texture.

Monkfish is an excellent alternative to hake or cod. In fact, vary the ingredients to accommodate whatever firm-fleshed and flaky fish or shellfish are available, but avoid mackerel and salmon, because they are too oily, and swordfish and tuna because their texture is too meaty.

deep-fried seafood
pescadito frito

*Andalusia is known as the 'frying pan of Spain',
because of the outstanding quality of the deep-fried
dishes throughout the region. So, it's no surprise
that all along the Mediterranean large and small
coastal restaurants feature platters piled high with
crisp fried seafood. The fish is always the catch of
the day, and few meals can be more enjoyable than
sitting under a parasol, sipping a chilled white wine
with a selection of fried prawns and squid rings.
You can also use this batter to fry whole baby
squid, whitebait and sardines. Romesco Sauce
(see page 233) and Garlic Mayonnaise (see page 232)
are both good for dipping the fried fish into.*

1 To make the batter, sift the flour and salt into a bowl
and make a well in the centre. Slowly add the water
and oil, stirring in the liquid until a smooth batter
forms; set aside to rest for at least 30 minutes.

2 Pour 7.5 cm/3 inches of oil into a large, heavy-based
frying pan over a high heat and heat until it reaches
190°C/375°F, or a cube of day-old bread browns in
30 seconds. Put the seasoned flour in a plastic bag.

3 Place the prawns in the bag and shake until they
are coated with flour. As you remove the prawns,
shake off any excess flour. Drop about 8 prawns in
the frying pan, without overcrowding it, and fry for
45 seconds. Turn them over with a large slotted spoon
and continue frying until the prawns are golden brown
and floating on the surface. Use a slotted spoon to
transfer them to crumpled kitchen paper and drain
very well. Sprinkle with salt and keep in a warm oven
while you fry the remainder.

4 Reheat the oil to the correct temperature between
batches and continue frying until all the seafood,
including the squid tentacles, is cooked. Garnish with
parsley and serve hot with lemon wedges.

SERVES 4–6
for the batter
125 g/4¹/₂ oz self-raising flour
¹/₂ tsp salt
150 ml/¹/₄ pint water
2 tbsp olive oil

olive oil, for deep-frying
**plain flour seasoned with salt and pepper and mild
  Spanish paprika, to taste**
**24 uncooked large prawns, peeled and deveined
  (see page 64)**
**2 large squid, prepared (see page 122), and cut into
  5-mm/¹/₄-inch thick rings**
reserved squid tentacles
salt
flat-leaved parsley, to garnish
lemon wedges, to serve

fish baked in salt
dorada a la sal

When temperatures rise in Palma, Majorca's capital, locals head to the picturesque harbour at Andratx for a relaxed Sunday meal. This dish is a speciality at the numerous small restaurants lining the harbour. The salt-encrusted fish is brought unceremoniously to the table in well-worn, battered roasting tins, where the salt crust is cracked and the moist fish is filleted and served.

Dorada, a member of the bream family, is a popular choice all along the Mediterranean, with a fine texture that makes it favoured by cooks. Unfortunately, it is only available in large fish markets away from the Mediterranean, so the best alternative is gilthead bream. (This fish gets its name from the 'gold' spot on either side of the head.) When it isn't available, try sea bream or sea bass.

SERVES 4

900 g/2 lb salt

140 g/5 oz plain flour

225 ml/8 fl oz water

1 dorada or gilthead bream, about 1 kg/2^1/4 lb, gutted
through the gills*

2 lemon slices

few sprigs fresh parsley

1 Preheat the oven to 230°C/450°F/Gas Mark 8. Mix the salt and flour in a bowl and make a well in the middle. Pour in the water to make a thick paste; set the mixture aside.

2 Push the lemon and parsley into the gill cavity. Use kitchen paper to wipe the fish dry. Cover the fish with the salt paste, using your hands. (It's not necessary to scale the fish before you add the paste, but do take care not to cut yourself.) Place in a roasting tin, making sure the fish is completely covered.

3 Roast the fish in the oven for 30 minutes. Remove from the oven and crack the crust. As you pull the crust back, it should bring the skin with it. Fillet the flesh and serve at once.

cook's tip

Gutting the fish through the gills keeps it in one piece, retaining both moisture and flavour. A fishmonger will do this for you, but with practice it can be done at home. Push back the flap over the gills and use your fingers to pull them out: be careful because they are sharp. Put your little finger into the cavity and use it to 'hook' the innards, then pull them out in one swift movement. Use a teaspoon to scrape out anything left behind. Rinse the fish inside and out under cold water, then pat dry with kitchen paper.

salt cod with mashed potatoes
brandada

Culinary folklore maintains there is a brandada *recipe for every day of the year. This is a legacy from the days when poor transportation meant salt cod was a dietary staple throughout the winter, as well as on Fridays and during Lent, when the Catholic Church prohibited all meat-eating. Although this preparation – with olive oil and mashed potatoes – has its origins in the south of France, it has crossed the border and is well established in Catalonia. Note that the dried salt cod (which you can find in Caribbean as well as Spanish food shops, if it isn't in your supermarket) needs to be soaked for up to 48 hours.* Pieces of salt cod are not always of a uniform consistency, but select the most even piece available so it will be tender and desalted throughout at the same time.*

SERVES 4–6

450 g/1 lb dried salt cod, broken into several pieces

4 lemon slices

4 sprigs fresh parsley

2 bay leaves

1 garlic clove, sliced

1/2 tsp fennel seeds

1/2 tsp black peppercorns, crushed lightly

500 g/1 lb 2 oz fluffy potatoes for mashing, such as
   King Edward, peeled and cut into chunks

about 4 tbsp garlic-flavoured olive oil

125 ml/4 fl oz milk

lemon juice, to taste

salt and pepper

1 Place the dried salt cod in a large bowl, cover with cold water and leave to soak for 48 hours, changing the water at least 3 times a day.

2 When you are ready to cook, put the lemon slices, parsley sprigs, bay leaves, garlic, fennel seeds and peppercorns in a saucepan with 1.2 litres/2 pints water over a high heat and bring to the boil. Reduce the heat and simmer for 45 minutes.

3 After the salt cod has soaked, transfer it to a large frying pan. Add enough of the flavoured liquid to cover and bring to the boil. Reduce the heat and simmer for 45 minutes, or until the fish is tender and flakes easily. Remove the fish from the water. Flake the flesh into fine pieces, removing all skin and tiny bones; set aside.

4 Meanwhile, cook the potatoes in a large saucepan of boiling salted water until tender; drain well. Put into a large bowl and mash, gradually beating in the flaked salt cod.

5 Put 4 tablespoons of the oil and the milk in a small saucepan over a medium heat and bring them to a simmer. Gradually beat into the salt cod mixture, adding extra until you achieve a consistency you like. Add lemon juice and salt and pepper to taste.

*cook's tip

Not all salt cod is the same, and some pieces can take longer than others to reconstitute and lose the excessive salty flavour. This makes it difficult to give an exact soaking time: it will be at least 24 hours and you should allow up to 48. When the texture loses its hardness, boil a small piece and taste to determine whether it needs to soak for longer

hake in white wine
merluza a la vasca

Spanish cooks are especially fond of using this meaty white-fleshed fish, not least because its mild, non-assertive flavour lends itself to combining with other ingredients. Its cod-like texture means it also can be fried, grilled, baked and steamed with excellent results.

This is a simple and popular dish from the Basque country, but sometimes a more elaborate dish is prepared including clams and prawns. Asparagus tips, French beans and peas are other tasty additions.

SERVES 4

about 2 tbsp plain flour

4 hake fillets, about 150 g/5 oz each

4 tbsp extra virgin olive oil

125 ml/4 fl oz dry white wine, such as a white Rioja

2 large garlic cloves, chopped very finely

6 spring onions, sliced finely

30 g/1 oz fresh parsley, chopped very finely

salt and pepper

1 Preheat the oven to 230°C/450°F/Gas Mark 8. Season the flour generously with salt and pepper on a flat plate. Dredge the skin side of the hake fillets in the seasoned flour, then shake off the excess; set aside.

2 Heat a shallow, flameproof casserole over a high heat until you can feel the heat rising. Add the oil and heat until a cube of day-old bread sizzles – it takes about 30 seconds. Add the hake fillets, skin side down, and cook for 3 minutes until the skin is golden brown.

3 Turn the fish over and season with salt and pepper to taste. Pour in the wine and add the garlic, spring onions and parsley. Transfer the casserole to the preheated oven, uncovered, and bake for 5 minutes, or until the flesh flakes easily. Serve the meal straight from the casserole.

variation

When hake isn't available, substitute cod.

salmon steaks with green sauce
salmón a la plancha con salsa verde

Wild salmon once thrived in northern rivers, but today Spanish cooks, like others throughout Europe, are more likely to buy farmed salmon. This flavour-packed sauce is ideal for perking up the mild taste of the fish, and also works well with grilled beef, veal, pork and chicken.

Sherry Rice (see page 243), Saffron Rice with Green Vegetables (see page 244) or Fried Potatoes (see page 247) are good accompaniments.

SERVES 4

for the Green Sauce

70 g/2^1/2 oz sprigs fresh flat-leaved parsley

8 large fresh basil leaves

2 sprigs fresh oregano, or ^{1}/2 tsp dried

3–4 anchovy fillets in oil, drained and chopped

2 tsp capers in brine, rinsed

1 shallot, chopped

1 large garlic clove

2–3 tsp lemon juice, to taste

125 ml/4 fl oz extra virgin olive oil

4 skinned salmon fillets, each about 150 g/5 oz

2 tbsp olive oil

salt and pepper

1 To make the Green Sauce, put the parsley, basil, oregano, anchovies, capers, shallot, garlic and lemon juice in a food processor or blender and process until chopped. With the motor running, slowly add the oil through the feed tube. Taste and adjust the seasoning, if necessary, remembering that the anchovies and capers can be salty. Pour into a serving bowl, cover with clingfilm and chill until required.*

2 When ready to serve, brush the salmon fillets on both sides with the olive oil and season with salt and pepper to taste. Heat a large frying pan until you can feel the heat rising from the surface. Add the salmon steaks and fry for 3 minutes. Flip the steaks over and continue frying for 2–3 minutes until they feel springy and the flesh flakes easily.

3 Serve the hot salmon steaks with a little of the chilled sauce spooned over.

*cook's tip
The Green Sauce can be prepared up to 2 days in advance and refrigerated until just before serving. The contrast of chilled sauce with hot rich salmon is excellent.

cod with spinach
bacalao a la catalana

The phrase a la Catalana *is an indication the dish will contain pine kernels and raisins. In trendy Barcelona restaurants this would be served simply with grilled tomato halves. It also goes well with Fried Potatoes (see page 247). A similar dish is made in the Balearic Islands, using Swiss chard rather than spinach.*

SERVES 4
for the Catalan spinach
55 g/2 oz raisins
55 g/2 oz pine kernels
4 tbsp extra virgin olive oil
3 garlic cloves, crushed
500 g/1 lb 2 oz baby spinach leaves, rinsed and shaken dry

4 cod fillets, each about 175 g/6 oz
olive oil
salt and pepper
lemon wedges, to serve

1 Put the raisins for the Catalan spinach in a small bowl, cover with hot water and set aside to soak for 15 minutes; drain well.

2 Meanwhile, put the pine kernels in a dry frying pan over a medium-high heat and dry-fry for 1–2 minutes, shaking frequently, until toasted and golden brown: watch closely because they burn quickly.

3 Heat the oil in a large, lidded frying pan over a medium-high heat. Add the garlic and fry for 2 minutes, or until golden, but not brown. Remove with a slotted spoon and discard.

4 Add the spinach to the oil with only the rinsing water clinging to its leaves. Cover and cook for 4–5 minutes until wilted. Uncover, stir in the drained raisins and pine kernels and continue cooking until all the liquid evaporates. Season to taste and keep warm.

5 To cook the cod, brush the fillets lightly with oil and sprinkle with salt and pepper. Place under a preheated hot grill about 10 cm/4 inches from the heat and grill for 8–10 minutes until the flesh is opaque and flakes easily.

6 Divide the spinach between 4 plates and place the cod fillets on top. Serve with lemon wedges.

Spain's food can be as colourful as some of its spectacular works of art

170 flounder for two
lenguado para dos

In northern Spain, especially around the port of La Coruña, flounder is prized for its tender, delicate flesh, which is suited to this technique of gentle roasting with wine. If flounder isn't available, use plaice or sole.

SERVES 2

150 ml/¹/₄ pint olive oil

375 g/13 oz waxy potatoes, peeled and sliced thinly

1 fennel bulb, trimmed and sliced thinly

2 large tomatoes, grilled and peeled, deseeded (see page 63), and chopped

2 shallots, sliced

salt and pepper

1 or 2 whole flounder, about 1.3 kg/3 lb, gutted

4 tbsp dry white wine

2 tbsp finely chopped fresh parsley

lemon wedges, to serve

1 Spread 4 tablespoons of the oil over the base in a shallow roasting tin large enough to hold the flounder. Arrange the potatoes in a single layer, then top with the fennel, tomatoes and shallots. Season with salt and pepper. Drizzle with a further 4 tablespoons of the oil. Roast the vegetables in a preheated oven, 200°C/400°F/Gas Mark 6, for 30 minutes.

2 Season the fish with salt and pepper and put on top of the vegetables. Sprinkle with the wine and the remaining 2 tablespoons of oil.

3 Return the roasting tin to the oven and roast the fish, uncovered, for 20 minutes, or until the flesh flakes easily. To serve, skin the fish and remove the fillets. Sprinkle the parsley over the vegetables. Arrange 2–4 fillets on each plate, with the vegetables spooned alongside, and the lemon wedges.

Water-features cool the squares and other public places of many Spanish cities

roasted tuna with orange and anchovies

atún asado con naranja y anchoas

Tuna is so abundant in the Strait of Gibraltar and off Spain's southern Atlantic coast that the waters near Cadiz are known as El Mar de Atún, the Tuna Sea. Tuna's rich, meaty flesh makes it ideal for roasting, and in this recipe one thick piece is treated like beef. Serve it with a simple accompaniment, such as Fried Potatoes (see page 247).

SERVES 4–6

200 ml/7 fl oz freshly squeezed orange juice

3 tbsp extra virgin olive oil

55 g/2 oz anchovy fillets in oil, chopped coarsely, with the oil reserved

small pinch dried chilli flakes, or to taste

pepper

1 tuna fillet, about 600 g/20 oz

1 Combine the orange juice, 2 tablespoons of the olive oil, the anchovies and their oil, the chilli flakes and pepper to taste in a non-metallic bowl large enough to hold the tuna. Add the tuna and spoon the marinade over it. Cover and chill for at least 2 hours to marinate, turning the tuna occasionally. Remove from the fridge 20 minutes before cooking to bring the fish up to room temperature.

2 Remove the tuna from the marinade and wipe dry. Heat the remaining tablespoon of olive oil in a large frying pan over a high heat. Add the tuna and sear for 1 minute on each side until lightly browned and crisp. Place the tuna in a small roasting tin and cover the tin tightly with foil.

3 Roast in a preheated oven, 220°C/425°F/Gas Mark 7, for 8 minutes for medium-rare and 10 minutes for medium-well done. Remove from the oven and set aside to rest for at least 2 minutes before carving.*

4 Meanwhile, put the marinade in a small saucepan over a high heat and bring to a rolling boil. Boil for at least 2 minutes.

5 Transfer the tuna to a serving platter and carve into thick slices, which will probably break into chunks as you cut them. Serve the sauce separately for spooning over. The tuna can be served hot or at room temperature, but the sauce is best hot.

*cook's tip

Just like beef, roasted tuna continues to cook after it comes out of the oven while it rests. An easy way to check whether the tuna is cooked is to insert a meat thermometer into it, through the foil, just before you put the covered tin in the oven. When the temperature reads 60°C/145°F the tuna will be medium.

174 paprika prawns
gambas al pimentón

*Simplicity itself, this recipe captures the flavour of
Spanish harbourside-eating where the* menú del dia
*is determined by the day's catch. Serve these piled
on a large platter and let everyone help themselves,
breaking off the heads and tails. A glass or two of
crisp white wine and plenty of crusty bread are the
ideal accompaniments.*

*For a summer lunch these are delicious served with
Orange and Fennel Salad (see page 109), or Sherry
Rice (see page 243).*

SERVES 4–6

16–24 large, uncooked tiger prawns

6 tbsp extra virgin olive oil

1 large garlic clove, crushed

$^1/_2$ tsp mild paprika, or to taste

salt

lemon wedges, to serve

1 Remove the shell from the middle of the prawns,
leaving the heads and tails intact. Devein the prawns
(see page 64).

2 Mix together the oil, garlic, paprika and salt in a
shallow dish large enough to hold the prawns in a
single layer. Stir together, then add the prawns and turn
so they are coated. Cover with clingfilm and marinate in
the fridge for at least 1 hour.

3 When ready to cook, heat a large, ridged cast-iron
griddle pan over a medium-high heat until you can
feel the heat rising. Add as many prawns as will fit
without over-crowding the griddle. Fry about 1 minute
until the prawns curl and the shells turn pink. Turn over
and continue frying for a further minute, or until
cooked through. Drain well on kitchen paper and keep
hot while you continue frying the remainder.

4 Serve at once with lemon wedges for squeezing
over the prawns.

variation

The marinated prawns are also delicious deep-fried.
Remove the heads and devein the prawns, then
marinate as above in step 2. Prepare the batter in the
recipe for Fried Pickled Monkfish (see page 55). Heat
enough olive oil in a large, heavy-based saucepan for
deep-frying until a cube of day-old bread sizzles – this
takes about 40 seconds. Dip the spicy prawns in the
batter, then fry for $1^1/_2$–2 minutes until curled and
golden brown. Cook in batches if necessary, to avoid
over-crowding the griddle. Sprinkle the prawns with
coarse sea salt and serve with lemon wedges for
squeezing over.

Eggs, be they baked, scrambled or fried, are always popular in Spain, and often served as a course on their own or as a light meal, such as the late evening meal. A la flamenca *refers to the colourful appearance of this popular dish. Vegetarian dishes are few and far between in Spain, but this one is easily adapted by omitting the chorizo.*

1 Heat the oil in a heavy-based frying pan over a medium-high heat. Add the peppers and onion and fry for 2 minutes, then add the garlic, chorizo and paprika and continue to fry for a further 3 minutes, or until the peppers and onion are soft, but not brown.

2 Stir in the tomatoes with their juices, the sugar and salt and pepper to taste and bring to the boil. Reduce the heat and simmer for about 10 minutes, uncovered.

3 Add the potatoes, beans and peas and continue simmering for 6–7 minutes until the potatoes are heated through and the beans and peas are cooked.

4 Divide the vegetable mixture between 4 small earthenware casseroles or individual serving dishes and adjust the seasoning if necessary. Crack an egg on top of each. Put in a preheated oven, 180°C/350°F/Gas Mark 4, and bake for 10 minutes, or until the yolks are set as desired. Serve at once.

cook's tip
Spaniards are exceptionally fond of canned vegetables, and this is one dish in which they are often used. Canned artichoke hearts, asparagus tips, diced carrots or turnips and peas are all suitable. Drain the vegetables well, then add them at the end of step 2 and skip step 3.

eggs on vegetables
huevos a la flamenca

177

SERVES 4

4 tbsp extra virgin olive oil

2 green peppers, cored, deseeded and chopped

1 large onion, chopped

2 garlic cloves, crushed

12 chorizo slices, each about 5 mm/^{1}/$_4$ inch thick, casings removed, if preferred

^{1}/$_4$ tsp Spanish mild or smoked paprika

800 g/1 lb 12 oz canned chopped tomatoes

pinch of sugar

salt and pepper

225 g/8 oz new potatoes, cooked and chopped into 1-cm/^{1}/$_2$-inch cubes*

100 g/3^1/$_2$ oz French or other green beans, chopped

100 g/3^1/$_2$ oz frozen or fresh shelled peas

4 large eggs

grilled pepper salad
ensalada de pimientos

Popular throughout the Mediterranean, this summer salad is ideal for serving on blazing hot days. To make it more substantial, add soaked and boiled salt cod (see page 162).

SERVES 4–6

6 large red, orange or yellow peppers, each cut in half lengthways, grilled and peeled (see page 74)

4 hard-boiled eggs, shelled

12 anchovy fillets in oil, drained

12 large black olives

extra virgin olive oil or garlic-flavoured olive oil

sherry vinegar

salt and pepper

country-style crusty bread, to serve

1 Remove any cores and seeds from the grilled peppers and cut into thin strips. Arrange on a serving platter.

2 Cut the eggs into wedges and arrange over the pepper strips, along with the anchovy fillets and olives.

3 Drizzle oil over the top, then splash with sherry vinegar, adding both to taste. Sprinkle a little salt and pepper over the top and serve with bread.

The cable car above Barcelona is a great way to see the city

tuna and bean salad
ensalada de atún y judías

SERVES 4–6

for the dressing

handful of fresh mint leaves, shredded

handful of fresh parsley leaves, chopped

1 garlic clove, crushed

4 tbsp extra virgin olive oil

1 tbsp red wine vinegar

salt and pepper

200 g/7 oz French or other green beans

400 g/14 oz canned small white beans, such as
  cannellini, rinsed and drained

4 spring onions, chopped finely

2 fresh tuna steaks, about 225 g/8 oz each and
  2 cm/³/4 inch thick

olive oil, for brushing

250 g/9 oz cherry tomatoes, halved

lettuce leaves

country-style crusty bread, to serve

mint and parsley leaves, to garnish

1 First, make the dressing. Put all the ingredients, with salt and pepper to taste, into a screw-top jar and shake until blended. Pour into a large bowl and set aside.

2 Bring a saucepan of lightly salted water to the boil. Add the beans and cook for 3 minutes. Add the white beans and continue cooking for about 4 minutes until the green beans are tender-crisp and the white

beans are heated through. Drain well and add to the bowl with the dressing, along with the spring onions; toss together.

3 To cook the tuna, heat a ridged griddle pan over a high heat. Lightly brush the tuna steaks with a little oil on one side, then put oiled side down on the griddle pan and fry for 2 minutes. Brush the top side with oil, then turn the steak over and continue frying for 2 minutes for rare or up to 4 minutes for well done.

4 Remove from the griddle pan and leave the tuna to stand for 2 minutes, or until completely cool. When ready to serve, add the tomatoes to the beans and toss lightly. Line a serving platter with lettuce leaves and pile on the bean salad. Flake the tuna over the top. Serve warm or at room temperature with plenty of bread, garnished with the herbs.

moors and christians
moros y cristianos

*From Valencia in the Levant, few Spanish dishes can
be as directly tied to historical events as this one:
the black beans represent the occupying Moors,
surrounded by the white rice representing the
Christians, who finally triumphed over the Arabs and
expelled them from the Iberian Peninsula.*

*Visit small villages in The Levant at the end of April
and you will come across Moros y Cristianos
festivals, with staged battles – and this dish, to
celebrate the victory.*

SERVES 4–6

for the rice

2 tbsp olive oil

400 g/14 oz Spanish short-grain rice, rinsed until the
    water runs clear

1 litre/1³⁄4 pints vegetable stock, not from a cube, hot

salt and pepper

for the beans

2 tbsp olive oil

55 g/2 oz serrano ham in one piece, diced, or prepared
    lardons

2 large green peppers, cored, deseeded and chopped
    finely

1 large onion, chopped finely

2 large garlic cloves, crushed

1 red chilli, deseeded and chopped finely, or to taste

800 g/1³⁄4 lb canned black beans, drained and rinsed

250 ml/9 fl oz vegetable stock, not from a cube

2 tbsp sherry vinegar

4 tbsp chopped fresh parsley

1 To make the rice, heat the oil in a shallow, heavy-
based flameproof casserole. Add the rice and stir
until it is coated in oil. Pour in the stock, season to taste
and bring to the boil. Reduce the heat and leave to
simmer for 20 minutes, uncovered and without stirring,
until most of the stock is absorbed and small holes
appear on the surface. If any liquid remains, cover,
remove from the heat and leave for 10 minutes.

2 Meanwhile, to make the beans, heat the oil in a
large frying pan or flameproof casserole. Add the
ham and fry for 2 minutes to flavour the oil. Add the
peppers and onion and fry for about 3 minutes, then
add the garlic and chilli and fry for a further 2 minutes,
or until the onion is softened, but not browned.

3 Stir in the beans and continue frying for
1–2 minutes. Add the stock and bring to the boil.
reduce the heat and simmer, uncovered, for about
10 minutes until the stock has evaporated and the
peppers are very tender. Taste and adjust the seasoning,
remembering that the ham can be salty; set aside.

4 Grease the inside of a 1.35-litre/2¹⁄4-pint ring
mould. Pack the rice into the mould, smoothing the
surface.* Reheat in a preheated oven, 150°C/300°F/Gas
Mark 2, for about 10 minutes. Reheat the beans, if
necessary, then stir in the sherry vinegar and parsley.

5 Using an oven glove, put a large serving plate face
down on top of the ring mould, then invert, giving a
sharp shake halfway over. Carefully lift off the mould.
Spoon the bean mixture into the centre and serve.

*cook's tip
Both the rice and the bean mixture can be prepared up
to a day in advance and chilled overnight in the fridge.
Remove the rice mould from the fridge at least
15 minutes before reheating as in step 4.

DESSERTS

186 Perhaps the most distinguishable feature of Spanish desserts is how few there are. Everyday meals at home are just as likely to end with fresh, juicy fruit, creamy sheep's cheese or a pot of yogurt.

With the Moorish occupation of Spain in AD 711 came the introduction of the exotic spices that are still used to flavour Spanish desserts, as well as the cornucopia of fruits – apricots, cherries, citrus fruits, figs, quince, passion fruit, peaches, plums and dates – that are enjoyed. The generous use of almonds both in desserts and confectionery is also inherited from the style of Arabic cooking. Poached Fruit, Seville Style (see page 215), 'Jewelled' Honey Mousses (see page 207) and Dates stuffed with Spanish Marzipan (see page 225) all reflect the glories of Moorish cuisine.

Yet the golden-topped, orange-flavoured Spanish Caramel Custard (see page 192), or *flan*, is universally popular, served both in homes and restaurants. Traditionally it is a baked, rich combination of eggs and milk, but in Valencia, the centre of Spain's orange-growing region, orange juice replaces some of the milk.

Another dessert whose popularity has spread through the country is *crema catalana*, Catalonia's version of the French *crème brûlée* – a dish of creamy custard with just a hint of lemon topped with a wafer-thin layer of crisp caramel (see page 195). There must be few people who don't enjoy the taste sensation of the creaminess combined with the slightly burnt-tasting caramel. (It is another point of contention with neighbouring France, but Spanish food historians maintain that Catalans were enjoying the burnt sugar topping for hundreds of years before *crème brûlée* appeared in any French cookery book.)

Some childhood desserts never fall out of fashion, and you won't find many Spanish adults who will turn down an offer of Fried Pastries (see page 221) or Fried Milk (see page 222).

Home-made ice cream is a perennially popular treat. Preserve the fresh flavour of the all-too-quick blood orange season in spring with Blood Orange Ice Cream (see page 204), a perfect dessert for a dinner party. Frozen Almond Cream (see page 201) is easy to make and ideal for anyone who is concerned about eating raw egg yolk, because it doesn't contain any. The hot chocolate sauce that accompanies this recipe is a good all-rounder to add a home-made touch to shop-bought ice cream.

Creamy Rice Pudding (see page 196) is a favourite from northern Cantabria. It is a versatile dessert for

Preserve the fresh flavour of the all-too-quick blood orange season in spring with Blood Orange Ice Cream, a perfect dessert for a dinner party

any time of year – serve it warm with extra cream for pouring over in winter, or chilled with a fresh fruit salad in the summer.

Lingering over a cup of coffee is a popular Spanish pastime, and Musicians' Bars (see page 224) and Dates Stuffed with Spanish Marzipan (see page 225) are after-dinner sweets that will always be appreciated. The Musicians' Bars are slabs of crisp caramel with dried fruit and mixed nuts pressed into it, and they make good hostess gifts to take to dinner parties.

Overleaf *The dry and dusty landscape of Spain's arid heart is home to vines and olives which almost bake in the heat*

192

spanish caramel custard
flan

This is possibly the best-known Spanish dessert outside Spain, which isn't surprising as it is probably the most popular in Spain. You'll find this on menus everywhere, although in Valencia it is often made with orange juice, rather than a custard base. What is common to most flan recipes, however, is the use of extra egg yolks, which give richness (sherry producers once clarified their product with egg whites, so clever cooks developed recipes that made the most of the leftover yolks).

SERVES 6

500 ml/18 fl oz full-fat milk

1/2 orange with 2 long, thin pieces of rind removed

1 vanilla pod, split, or 1/2 tsp vanilla extract

175 g/6 oz caster sugar

butter, for greasing the dish

3 large eggs, plus 2 large egg yolks

1 Pour the milk into a saucepan with the orange rind and vanilla pod or extract. Bring to the boil, then remove from the heat and stir in 100 g/3 1/2 oz of the sugar; set aside for at least 30 minutes to infuse.

2 Meanwhile, put the remaining 75 g/2 3/4 oz of sugar and 4 tablespoons of water in another saucepan over a medium-high heat. Stir until the sugar dissolves, then boil without stirring until the caramel turns deep golden brown.

3 Immediately remove the saucepan from the heat and squeeze in a few drops of orange juice to stop the cooking. Pour into a lightly buttered 1.2-litre/2-pint soufflé dish and swirl to cover the base; set aside.

4 When the milk has infused, return the saucepan to the heat and bring the milk to a simmer. Beat the whole eggs and egg yolks together in a heatproof bowl. Pour the warm milk into the eggs, whisking constantly. Strain this mixture into the soufflé dish.

5 Place the soufflé dish in a roasting tin and pour in enough boiling water to come halfway up the sides of the dish. Bake in a preheated oven, 160°C/325°F/Gas Mark 3, for 75–90 minutes until set and a knife inserted in the centre comes out clean.

6 Remove the soufflé dish from the roasting tin and set aside to cool completely. Cover and chill overnight.

7 To serve, run a metal spatula around the side of the dish, then invert onto a serving plate with a rim, shaking firmly to release.

San Sebastian is a thriving cultural centre and a popular destination for tourists

catalan burnt cream
crema catalana

This classic rich, creamy dessert with its 'burnt' sugar topping is from Catalonia. Outward appearances lead one to think this is the same as the French crème brûlée, *but the difference lies under the crisp, caramelized topping. Unlike its French cousin, this pudding isn't baked, so it remains runny. Prepare the custard at least 12 hours in advance, to allow it to thicken in the fridge.*

SERVES 6

750 ml/24 fl oz full-fat milk

1 vanilla pod, split

thinly pared rind of $^1/_2$ lemon

7 large egg yolks

200 g/7 oz caster sugar

3 tbsp cornflour

1 Prepare the custard a day in advance of serving. Pour the milk into a saucepan with the vanilla pod and lemon rind. Bring to the boil, then remove from the heat and set aside for at least 30 minutes to infuse.

2 Select a heatproof bowl that will fit over a saucepan without touching the bottom. Put the eggs and 100 g/3$^1/_2$ oz sugar in the bowl and beat until the sugar dissolves and the mixture is thick and creamy.

3 Return the infused milk to the heat and bring to a simmer. Stir 4 tablespoons of the warm milk into a small bowl with the cornflour, stirring until a smooth paste forms. Stir this paste into the simmering milk and stir over a medium-low heat for 1 minute.

4 Strain the milk into the egg mixture and whisk until well blended. Rinse out the saucepan and put a small amount of water in the bottom. Place the saucepan over a medium-high heat and bring the water to a simmer. Reduce the heat, put the bowl on top and stir for 25–30 minutes until the custard is thick enough to coat the

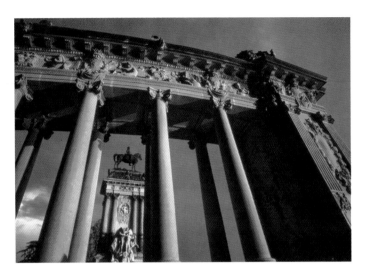

Classical grandeur abounds in Madrid in the form of carved columns and statues

back of the spoon; the water must not touch the base of the bowl or the eggs might scramble.

5 Divide the mixture between 6 x 10-cm/4-inch round earthenware serving dishes called *cazuelas* or flat, white French *crème brûlée* dishes. Leave to cool completely, then cover and chill for at least 12 hours.

6 To serve, sprinkle the top of each with a thin layer of caster sugar. In Catalonia, the tops are caramelized with a special flat iron that is heated in a gas flame and then placed on top of the sugar. Unless you happen to have one of these, use a kitchen blow torch; a grill isn't hot enough. Leave to stand while the caramel hardens, then serve. The caramel will remain firm for about 1 hour at room temperature; do not return to the fridge or the caramel will 'melt'.

196

rice pudding
arroz con leche

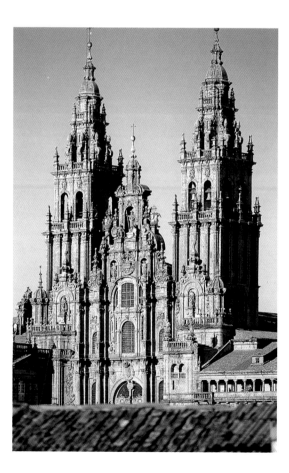

*Northern Cantabria produces some of Spain's
richest dairy products, so it is not surprising that
the region's versions of this popular, comforting
dessert are made with large quantities of full-fat
milk. This is a thick, creamy pudding that tastes
equally good warmed or chilled. It can also be served
with light brown sugar sprinkled over the top, or
with Poached Fruit, Seville Style (see page 215), or
with chopped Caramelized Almonds (see page 96)
instead of the sugar.*

SERVES 4–6

1 large orange

1 lemon

1 litre/1³/₄ pints milk

250 g/9 oz Spanish short-grain rice

100 g/3¹/₂ oz caster sugar

1 vanilla pod, split

pinch of salt

125 ml/4 fl oz double cream

light brown sugar, to serve (optional)

1 Finely grate the rinds from the orange and lemon; set
aside. Rinse a heavy-based saucepan with cold water
and do not dry it.

2 Put the milk and rice in the saucepan over a medium-
high heat and bring to the boil. Reduce the heat
and stir in the caster sugar, vanilla pod, orange and
lemon rinds and salt and simmer, stirring frequently,
until the pudding is thick and creamy and the rice
grains are tender: this can take up to 30 minutes,
depending on how wide the saucepan is.

3 Remove the vanilla pod and stir in the cream.
Serve at once, sprinkled with light brown sugar, if
desired, or leave to cool completely, cover and chill until
required. (The pudding will thicken as it cools, so stir in
extra milk, if necessary.)

*Architecture on such a grand scale
is testimony to Spain's rich history*

rich chocolate cake
pastel de chocolate

Rich chocolate cakes, such as this, are ideal to enjoy with midmorning coffee or afternoon tea. It's not unusual to see cakes sitting on top of Spanish bars for when customers stop in for a cup of coffee, rather than a beer or sherry.

This cake keeps for up to 4 days wrapped in foil.

MAKES 10–12 SLICES

100 g/3^1/$_2$ oz raisins

finely grated rind and juice of 1 orange

175 g/6 oz butter, diced, plus extra for greasing the tin

100 g/3^1/$_2$ oz plain chocolate, at least 70% cocoa solids, broken up

4 large eggs, beaten

100 g/3^1/$_2$ oz caster sugar

1 tsp vanilla essence

55 g/2 oz plain flour

55 g/2 oz ground almonds

^{1}/$_2$ tsp baking powder

pinch salt

55 g/2 oz blanched almonds, lightly toasted and chopped

icing sugar, sifted, to decorate

1 Put the raisins in a small bowl, add the orange juice and leave to soak for 20 minutes. Line a deep 25-cm/10-inch round cake tin with a removable base with greaseproof paper and grease the paper; set aside.

2 Melt the butter and chocolate together in a small saucepan over a medium heat, stirring. Remove from the heat and set aside to cool.

3 Using an electric mixer beat the eggs, sugar and vanilla together for about 3 minutes until light and fluffy. Stir in the cooled chocolate mixture.

4 Drain the raisins if they haven't absorbed all the orange juice. Sift over the flour, ground almonds, baking powder and salt. Add the raisins, orange rind and almonds and fold everything together.

5 Spoon into the cake tin and smooth the surface. Bake in a preheated oven, 180°C/350°F/Gas Mark 4, for about 40 minutes, or until a cocktail stick inserted into the centre comes out clean and the cake starts to come away from the side of the tin. Leave to cool in the tin for 10 minutes, then remove from the tin and allow to cool completely on a wire rack. Dust the surface with icing sugar before serving.

frozen almond cream with hot chocolate sauce

crema de almendras con salsa de chocolate

SERVES 4–6

175 g/6 oz blanched almonds (see page 50)

300 ml/^{1}/$_2$ pint double cream

^{1}/$_4$ tsp almond essence

150 ml/^{1}/$_4$ pint single cream

55 g/2 oz icing sugar

for the Hot Chocolate Sauce

100 g/3^1/$_2$ oz plain chocolate, broken into pieces

3 tbsp golden syrup

4 tbsp water

25 g/1 oz unsalted butter, diced

^{1}/$_4$ tsp vanilla essence

1 Place the blanched almonds on a baking sheet and toast in a preheated oven, 200°C/400°F/Gas Mark 6, for 8–10 minutes, stirring occasionally, until golden brown and giving off a 'toasted' aroma: watch carefully after 7 minutes because they burn quickly. Immediately pour onto a chopping board and leave to cool. Coarsely chop 55 g/2 oz by hand, and finely grind the remainder; set both aside separately.

2 Whip the double cream with the almond essence until soft peaks form. Stir in the single cream and continue whipping, sifting in the icing sugar in 3 batches. Transfer to an ice-cream maker and freeze following the manufacturer's instructions.* When the cream is almost frozen, transfer it to a bowl, and stir in the chopped almonds so they are evenly distributed.

3 Put the cream mixture in a 450-g/1-lb loaf tin and smooth the top. Wrap tightly in foil and put in the freezer for at least 3 hours.

4 To make the hot chocolate sauce, place a heatproof bowl over a saucepan of simmering water. Add the chocolate, syrup and water and stir until the chocolate melts. Stir in the butter and vanilla essence until smooth.

5 To serve, unwrap the tin and dip the base in a sink of boiling water for just a couple of seconds. Invert onto a freezerproof tray, giving a sharp shake until the frozen cream drops out. Using a palette knife, coat the top and sides with the finely chopped almonds; return to the freezer unless serving at once.

6 Use a warm knife to slice into 8–12 slices. Arrange 2 slices on each plate and spoon the hot chocolate sauce around.

*cook's tips

If you don't have an ice cream maker, put the mixture in a freezerproof container and freeze for 2 hours, or until it is starting to thicken and set around the edge. Beat well and return to the freezer until almost frozen. Stir in the almonds and proceed with step 3.

You can make the sauce and the dessert in advance. Remove the dessert from the freezer 15 minutes before serving, and reheat the sauce gently.

202

creamy chocolate puddings
pudíns de chocolate

SERVES 4–6

175 g/6 oz plain chocolate, at least 70% cocoa
   solids, broken up

1 1/2 tbsp orange juice

3 tbsp water

25 g/1 oz unsalted butter, diced

2 eggs, separated

1/8 tsp cream of tartar

3 tbsp caster sugar

6 tbsp double cream

for the Pistachio-orange Praline

sunflower oil, for greasing

55 g/2 oz caster sugar

55 g/2 oz shelled pistachio nuts

finely grated rind of 1 large orange

1 Melt the chocolate with the orange juice and water in a small saucepan over a very low heat, stirring constantly. Remove from the heat and stir in the butter until melted and incorporated. Using a rubber spatula, scrape the chocolate into a bowl.

2 Beat the egg yolks until blended, then beat them into the chocolate mixture; set aside to cool.

3 In a clean bowl, whisk the egg whites with the cream of tartar until soft peaks form. Gradually beat in the sugar, 1 tablespoon at a time, beating well after each addition, until the meringue is glossy. Beat 1 tablespoon of the meringue mixture into the chocolate mixture, then fold in the rest.

4 In a separate bowl, whip the cream until soft peaks form: do not make it too stiff. Fold into the chocolate mixture. Spoon into individual glass bowls or wine glasses, or 1 large serving bowl. Cover with clingfilm and chill for at least 4 hours.

5 Meanwhile, make the praline. Lightly grease a baking sheet with sunflower oil; set aside. Put the sugar and pistachios in a small saucepan over a medium heat. When the sugar starts to melt, stir gently until a liquid caramel forms and the nuts start popping.

6 Pour the praline onto the baking sheet and immediately finely grate the orange rind over. Leave to cool until firm. Coarsely chop or finely grind, according to your liking. Cover tightly and store at room temperature until required.

7 Just before serving, sprinkle the praline over the chocolate pudding.

variations
Soak the raisins in Spanish brandy or sherry instead of the orange juice. The praline can also be made with blanched almonds or hazelnuts.

blood orange ice cream
helado de naranjas de sangre

The Almond Biscuits (see page 216) go well with this rich, creamy ice cream.

SERVES 4–6

3 large blood oranges, washed

85 ml/3 fl oz semi-skimmed milk

85 ml/3 fl oz single cream

125 g/4^1/$_2$ oz caster sugar

4 large egg yolks

450 ml/16 fl oz double cream

^{1}/$_8$ tsp vanilla essence

1 Thinly pare the rind from 2 of the oranges, reserving a few strips for decoration, and finely grate the rind from the third. Squeeze the oranges to give 125 ml/ 4 fl oz juice; set aside.

2 Pour the milk and cream into a saucepan with the pared orange rind. Bring to the boil, then remove from the heat; set aside for at least 30 minutes to infuse.

3 Select a heatproof bowl that fits over the saucepan without touching the bottom. Put the sugar and egg yolks in the bowl and beat until thick and creamy.

4 Return the milk mixture to the heat and bring to a simmer. Pour the milk onto the eggs and whisk until well blended. Wash the saucepan and put a small amount of water in the bottom. Place over a medium heat and bring the water to a simmer. Reduce the heat. Put the bowl on top and stir for about 20 minutes until a thick custard forms that coats the back of the spoon; the water must not touch the bottom of the bowl or the eggs might scramble.

5 Strain the mixture into a clean bowl. Stir in the finely grated orange rind and set aside for 10 minutes.

6 Stir in the reserved juice, double cream and vanilla essence. Transfer to an ice cream maker and freeze following the manufacturer's instructions. (Alternatively, strain the mixture into a freezerproof container and freeze for 2 hours, or until mushy and freezing around the edges. Tip into a bowl and beat. Return to the freezer and repeat the process twice more.) Remove from the freezer to soften 15 minutes before serving. Decorate with strips of the reserved rind.

The usual haunts for tourists may not be where to find the best bars and restaurants: follow the locals!

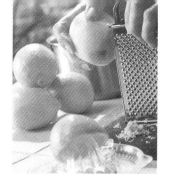

lemon sorbet with cava
sorbete de limón con cava

Once you have frozen the sorbet, this is an almost-instant dinner-party dessert. The sorbet will maintain its fresh flavour for up to a month in the freezer.

SERVES 4–6
3–4 lemons
250 ml/9 fl oz water
200 g/7 oz caster sugar
1 bottle Spanish cava, chilled, to serve

1 Roll the lemons on the work surface, pressing firmly, which helps to extract as much juice as possible. Pare off a few strips of rind and reserve for decoration, then finely grate the rind from 3 lemons. Squeeze the juice from as many of the lemons as necessary to give 175 ml/6 fl oz.

2 Put the water and sugar in a heavy-based saucepan over a medium-high heat and stir to dissolve the sugar. Bring to the boil, without stirring, and boil for 2 minutes. Remove from the heat, stir in the lemon rind, cover and leave to stand for 30 minutes, or until cool.

3 When the mixture is cool, stir in the lemon juice. Strain into an ice cream maker and freeze according to the manufacturer's instructions. (Alternatively, strain the mixture into a freezerproof container and freeze for 2 hours, or until mushy and freezing around the edges. Tip into a bowl and beat. Return to the freezer and repeat the process twice more.) Remove the sorbet from the freezer to soften 10 minutes before serving.

4 To serve, scoop into 4–6 tall glasses, decorate with the reserved rind, if using, and top up with cava.

variation
Spaniards also serve lemon sorbet in frozen hollow lemon shells. To do this, slice the tops off 4–6 lemons and use a sharp teaspoon to scoop out the fruit. Spoon the almost-frozen sorbet into the lemons and place in the freezer upright until frozen.

'jewelled' honey mousses

mousse de miel adornado

SERVES 6

1 large egg, plus 3 large egg yolks

175 g/6 oz honey

300 ml/¹/₂ pint double cream

3 pomegranates, to serve

1 Line 6 ramekins with pieces of clingfilm large enough to extend over the tops; set aside.

2 Put the whole egg, egg yolks and honey in a large bowl and beat until blended and fluffy. Put the double cream in another bowl and beat until stiff peaks form. Fold the cream into the egg-and-honey mixture.

3 Equally divide the mixture between the ramekins, then fold the excess clingfilm over the top of each. Place in the freezer for at least 8 hours until firm. These mousses can be served directly from the freezer, because the texture isn't solid.

4 To serve, unfold the clingfilm, then invert each ramekin onto a serving plate and remove the ramekin and clingfilm. Cut the pomegranates in half and hold one half over a mousse in turn. Use your other hand to tap firmly on the base of the pomegranate, so the seeds fall over the mousse. Serve at once.

Overleaf *The Moorish influence on architecture is apparent in many Spanish urban landscapes*

baked apricots with honey
albaricoques al horno con miel

SERVES 4

butter, for greasing

4 apricots, each cut in half and stoned

4 tbsp flaked almonds

4 tbsp honey

pinch ground ginger or grated nutmeg

vanilla ice cream, to serve (optional)

1 Lightly butter an ovenproof dish large enough to hold the apricot halves in a single layer.

2 Arrange the apricot halves in the dish, cut sides up. Sprinkle with the almonds and drizzle the honey over. Dust with the spice.

3 Bake in a preheated oven, 200°C/400°F/Gas Mark 6, for 12–15 minutes until the apricots are tender and the almonds golden. Remove from the oven and serve at once, with ice cream on the side, if desired.

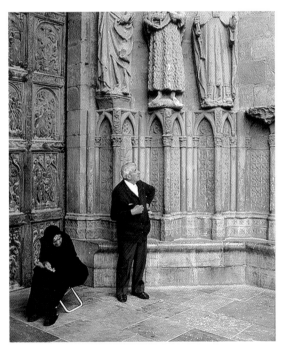

Few can fail to be overawed by the splendour of church architecture and detailing

212

valencia caramel oranges
naranjas de valencia con caramelo

Vast orange groves in and around Valencia supply Europe with the juicy fruit. This simple dessert can be prepared up to a day ahead and chilled until required. It is a refreshing end to a meal and delicious served on its own or spooned over vanilla or chocolate ice cream.

SERVES 4–6

4 large, juicy oranges

250 g/9 oz caster sugar

300 ml/¹/₂ pint water

4–6 tbsp flaked almonds, toasted, to serve

1 Working over a heatproof bowl to catch any juices, and using a small serrated knife, pare the oranges, taking care not to leave any of the bitter-tasting pith. Use the knife to remove the orange segments, cutting between the membranes. Squeeze the empty membranes over the bowl to extract as much juice as possible; discard the membranes and set the segments and juice aside.

2 Put the sugar and 150 ml/¹/₄ pint of the water into a small, heavy-based saucepan over a medium-high heat. Stir until the sugar dissolves, then bring to the boil and boil, without stirring, until the syrup turns a rich golden brown.

3 Pour the remaining water into the saucepan (stand back because the caramel will splatter). Stir again until the caramel dissolves. Remove from the heat and leave the caramel to cool slightly, then pour over the oranges. Stir to blend the orange juice into the caramel. Leave the oranges to cool completely, then cover with clingfilm and chill for at least 2 hours before serving.

4 Just before serving, sprinkle the caramel oranges with the toasted flaked almonds.

poached fruit, seville style
frutas escalfadas a la sevillana

The Moorish influence on Spanish cuisine is so evident in Andalusia, with the generous use of fruit and spices. Tender, juicy apricots are used in this recipe, but many other tree fruits, such as pears or nectarines, are also delicious. The fruit and syrup can be served on their own, or with vanilla ice cream, Rice Pudding (see page 196) or Fried Pastries (see page 221).

SERVES 4–6

for the syrup

1/2 tsp fennel seeds

1/2 tsp coriander seeds

1/4 tsp black peppercorns

200 g/7 oz caster sugar

225 m/8 fl oz red wine, such as Rioja

225 ml/8 fl oz water

3 tbsp freshly squeezed orange juice

2 tbsp freshly squeezed lemon juice

2 tbsp Spanish cream sherry

3 cloves

1 cinnamon stick

12 tender apricots, halved and stoned

2 tbsp flaked almonds, toasted, to decorate

1 First, make the red wine syrup. Put the fennel, coriander seeds and peppercorns in a heavy-based saucepan over a high heat and dry-fry for up to about 1 minute until they start to give off an aroma. Immediately tip them out of the saucepan to stop the cooking. Put in a mortar and lightly crush.

2 Put the sugar, wine, water, orange and lemon juices, sherry and all the spices into a heavy-based saucepan over a medium-high heat, stirring to dissolve the sugar. Bring to the boil, without stirring, and allow to bubble for 5 minutes.

3 Add the fruit and simmer for 6–8 minutes until tender. Remove the saucepan from the heat and transfer to a bowl of iced water and leave to cool. When cool enough to handle, remove the apricots and peel. Cover and chill until required.

4 Meanwhile, return the juices to the heat and boil until the syrup thickens and the flavours become more concentrated. Remove from the heat and leave to cool.

5 When ready to serve, place the fruit in serving bowls, spoon the syrup over, then sprinkle with flaked almonds.

216 # almond biscuits
galletas de almendras

Rich almond biscuits like these are eaten at Easter, and pastry shops will have tempting trays of them on display in their windows.

MAKES ABOUT 60

150 g/5^{1}/$_{2}$ oz butter, at room temperature

150 g/5^{1}/$_{2}$ oz caster sugar

115 g/4 oz plain flour

25 g/1 oz ground almonds

pinch of salt

75 g/2^{3}/$_{4}$ oz blanched almonds (see page 50), toasted
   lightly and chopped finely

finely grated rind of 1 large lemon

4 medium egg whites

1 Put the butter and sugar into a bowl and beat until light and fluffy. Sift over the flour, ground almonds and salt, tipping in any ground almonds left in the sieve. Use a large metal spoon to fold in the chopped almonds and lemon rind.

2 In a separate, spotlessly clean bowl, whisk the egg whites until soft peaks form. Fold the egg whites into the almond mixture.

3 Drop small teaspoonfuls of the biscuit mixture onto 1 or more well-greased baking sheets, spacing them well apart. (You might need to cook in batches.) Bake in a preheated oven, 180°C/350°F/Gas Mark 4, for 15–20 minutes until golden brown on the edges. Transfer to a wire rack to cool completely. Continue baking until all the mixture is used. Store in an airtight container for up to 1 week.

Fresh, colourful market produce is carried away daily, somewhere – somehow – in every Spanish town and city

218

almond tart
tarta de santiago

Almond tarts are not just served for dessert in Spain – chances are you'll find one at any takeaway coffee shop, where it will be enjoyed with the endless cups of coffee drunk during the day. The tart's popularity reaches a peak in Santiago de Compostela, home of the cathedral of St James, which thousands of pilgrims visit each year, carrying scallop shells as the symbol of the saint. Silver templates are used to mark the cross of St James on the icing sugar-covered tarts in the city, but an upturned scallop shell makes a good alternative. Position a cleaned scallop shell in the centre of the tart and heavily dredge icing sugar over the surface. Carefully remove the shell to reveal its impression.

MAKES 1 x 25-CM/10-INCH TART

for the pastry

280 g/10 oz plain flour

150 g/5^1/$_2$ oz caster sugar

1 tsp finely grated lemon rind

pinch of salt

150 g/5^1/$_2$ oz unsalted butter, chilled and cut into
  small dice

1 medium egg, beaten lightly

1 tbsp chilled water

175 g/6 oz unsalted butter, at room temperature

175 g/6 oz caster sugar

3 large eggs

175 g/6 oz finely ground almonds

2 tsp plain flour

1 tbsp finely grated orange rind

^{1}/$_2$ tsp almond essence

icing sugar, to decorate

crème fraîche (optional), to serve

1 First, make the pastry. Put the flour, sugar, lemon rind and salt in a bowl. Rub or cut in the butter until the mixture resembles fine breadcrumbs. Combine the egg and water, then slowly pour into the flour, stirring with a fork until a rough mass forms. Shape into a ball and chill for at least 1 hour.

2 Roll out the pastry on a lightly floured surface* until 3 mm/^{1}/$_8$ inch thick. Use to line a greased 25-cm/10-inch tart tin with a removable base. Return the tart tin to the fridge for at least 15 minutes.

3 Cover the pastry case with foil and fill the tart with baking beans or dried pulses. Place in a preheated oven, 220°C/425°F/Gas Mark 7, and bake for 12 minutes. Remove the beans and foil and return the pastry case to the oven for 4 minutes to dry the base. Remove from the oven and reduce the oven temperature to 200°C/400°F/Gas Mark 6.

4 Meanwhile, make the filling. Beat the butter and sugar until creamy. Beat in the eggs, 1 at a time. Add the almonds, flour, orange rind and almond extract and beat until blended.

5 Spoon the filling into the pastry case and smooth the surface. Bake for 30–35 minutes until the top is golden and the tip of a knife inserted in the centre comes out clean. Leave to cool completely on a wire rack, then dust the top with sifted icing sugar (see introduction). Serve with a spoonful of crème fraîche, if desired.

cook's tip

If you have difficulty rolling out this rich pastry, roll it between two sheets of clingfilm. Pull off the top sheet, invert the pastry into the tin and peel off the second sheet. Alternatively, roll out the dough in small pieces and 'patch' them together with lightly floured fingers.

fried pastries
pasteles fritos

A treat for children of all ages!

MAKES 16–20

100 g/3^1/$_2$ oz plain flour

40 g/1^1/$_2$ oz unsalted butter, melted

1 tbsp Spanish cream sherry

^{1}/$_2$ tsp vanilla essence

pinch of salt

1 small egg, beaten very lightly

olive oil, for deep-frying

to decorate

2 tbsp icing sugar

^{1}/$_2$ tsp ground cinnamon

pinch of ground ginger

1 Put the flour in a bowl and make a well in the centre. Add the butter, cream sherry, vanilla extract, salt and 1 tablespoon of the egg, and mix together until a dough forms. Knead the dough in the bowl until it is smooth. Shape into a ball and wrap in clingfilm; set aside at room temperature for 15 minutes.

2 On a lightly floured surface roll out half the dough very thinly. Use a 5.5-cm/2^1/$_4$-inch fluted biscuit cutter and cut out 8–10 circles, re-rolling the trimmings. Repeat with the remaining dough.

3 Heat 5 cm/2 inches oil in a heavy-based frying pan over a high heat to 180°C/350°F or until a cube of day-old bread turns brown in 35 seconds. Add 5–6 dough circles, without overcrowding the saucepan, and fry for 45 seconds, turn them over with a large slotted spoon, and continue frying until the circles are puffed on both sides and golden brown. Transfer to crumpled kitchen paper and drain very well. Take care: they are delicate and can break easily. Repeat with the remaining dough circles.

4 While the pastries are still hot, mix the icing sugar, cinnamon and ginger together. Use a fine sieve and sift the mixture over the warm pastries. These will keep in an airtight container for up to 3 days.

222

fried milk
leche frita

MAKES ABOUT 25

groundnut or other flavourless oil

600 ml/1 pint full-fat milk

1 cinnamon stick

1 strip of lemon rind, without any white pith

2 large eggs plus 1 large egg yolk

100 g/3^1/$_2$ oz caster sugar

55 g/2 oz plain flour, plus extra for dusting

35 g/1^1/$_4$ oz cornflour

1 tsp vanilla extract

olive oil

extra caster sugar and cinnamon, to decorate

1 Line a 30 x 23-cm/12 x 9-inch baking tray with foil and lightly grease with the oil; set aside.

2 Pour the milk into a saucepan with the cinnamon stick and lemon rind. Bring to the boil, then remove from the heat; set aside for at least 30 minutes to infuse.

3 Put the eggs, egg yolk, sugar, flour, cornflour and vanilla extract in the bowl and beat until smooth.

4 Return the milk mixture to the heat and bring to a simmer. Pour the milk onto the egg mixture and whisk until well blended. Bring to the boil, stirring, then reduce the heat and simmer for 2–3 minutes until the custard thickens and leaves the side of the saucepan.

5 Pour the custard into the prepared baking tray and use a wet spatula to smooth the surface. Leave to cool completely, then cover and chill for 2–3 hours.

6 Invert the custard onto a chopping board and peel off the foil. Cut on the diagonal to make 25 triangles, plus odd pieces of trimming from the edges. Dust the custard triangles in flour and shake off any excess.

7 Heat 5 cm/2 inches of oil in a heavy-based sauté pan or frying pan over a high heat to 180°C/350°F, or until a cube of day-old bread browns in 35 seconds. Add 5–6 custard triangles at a time, without over-crowding the frying pan, and fry for 45 seconds. Turn them over with a fish slice or slotted spoon; continue frying until golden brown. Transfer to crumpled kitchen paper and drain well. Repeat in batches with the remaining triangles. Serve sprinkled with the extra sugar and cinnamon.

Urban Spaniards retain their love of regional cuisine and top-quality ingredients, despite their modern lifestyle

musicians' bars
de musico

These brittle fruit-and-nut bars take their name from the time when troupes of musicians travelled through Spain, performing for festivals and weddings or giving impromptu concerts. Their meagre wages might have been a meal, a bed for the night, or whatever dried fruit and nuts were available to provide sustenance on the following day's travels. Today, the culinary legacy is that any tarts or caramel slabs with a mixed fruit-and-nut topping are known as de musico, *or musicians' desserts.*

MAKES 3 BARS; EACH BAR SERVES 4–6

500 g/1 lb 2 oz caster sugar

150 ml/¼ pint water

⅛ tsp white wine vinegar

groundnut or other flavourless oil, for greasing

300 g/10½ oz mixed nuts, such as blanched or unblanched almonds, flaked almonds, skinned hazelnuts, salted or unsalted skinned peanuts and salted or unsalted pecans

100 g/3½ oz raisins

55 g/2 oz ready-to-eat dried apricots, figs or dates, chopped very finely

55 g/2 oz pine kernels

1 Put the sugar, water and vinegar in a heavy-based saucepan over a medium-high heat, stirring to dissolve the sugar. Bring to the boil, then boil, without stirring, for 20–25 minutes until the caramel reaches 175°C/350°F on a sugar thermometer, or turns a rich amber colour.

2 Meanwhile, generously grease a 30 x 23-cm/ 12 x 9-inch baking tin, and a large chef's knife with the oil; set both aside. Combine the nuts and fruit in a bowl.

3 When the caramel is amber coloured, stir in the fruit and nuts and immediately pour into the prepared baking tin. Work very quickly, using a wet spatula to spread the mixture evenly.

4 Leave the caramel for a few minutes to set until firm but not too brittle to cut. Invert the caramel bar onto a sheet of greased greaseproof paper and use the oiled knife to cut into 3 slabs each measuring 10 x 23 cm/4 x 9 inches. Leave to cool until brittle, then wrap each in foil and store for up to 1 week.

dates stuffed with spanish marzipan
dátiles rellenos de melindres

Elche, near Alicante on the Costa Blanca, has had glorious date palms for the past 3,000 years, so it's no surprise that dates are teamed with marzipan, reflecting the Moorish contribution to Spanish food. Spanish marzipan differs from that made in northern Europe as it contains no egg white. The possible flavourings are almost endless: try finely grated orange or lemon rind, very finely chopped crystallised fruit, or add finely chopped pistachio nuts.

MAKES 12–14

for the Spanish Marzipan

70 g/2^1/$_2$ oz icing sugar, plus a little extra for dusting

70 g/2^1/$_2$ oz ground almonds

^{1}/$_4$ tsp almond essence

12–14 ready-to-eat dates

1 To make the Spanish marzipan, sift the icing sugar then mix with the ground almonds in a bowl. Sprinkle over the almond essence. Gradually add a little water, ^{1}/$_4$ teaspoon at a time, until the mixture comes together and can be pressed into a ball.

2 Knead the marzipan with your hands and then on a work surface lightly dusted with icing sugar until it is smooth. It is now ready to be used, or can be wrapped in clingfilm and stored in the fridge for up to 3 days.

3 To stuff the dates, use a small knife to slice along the length of each, then open out and pull out the stone. Break off a small piece of the marzipan and mould it into a 'log', pressing it into the date. Arrange the dates on a plate and serve with coffee after dinner.

ACCOMPANIMENTS & DRINKS

Simplicity is one of the hallmarks of Spanish meals, and complicated sauces do not feature widely.

In Catalonia, Romesco Sauce (see page 233), with toasted almonds, tomatoes and hot, sweet dried chillies, has been transformed from being the base of a mixed seafood stew from the coastal town of Tarragona to a sauce that can be served with grilled or baked seafood. (It also livens up a roast chicken and grilled pork chops, even if this pairing is somewhat unconventional.)

In the Canary Islands the sauce to accompany the tapas 'Wrinkled' Potatoes (see page 84) is *mojo rojo*, a bright red sauce, traditionally made with hot Spanish paprika and *pimientos del piquillo*. It is just as good with meatballs (see page 77). A green version, *mojo verde*, is flavoured with coriander.

The piquant garlic-flavoured mayonnaise, *allioli*, on the other hand, has a long history, and Spanish food historians claim that it is the forerunner of French mayonnaise. The name literally means 'garlic and oil'. Its pungency depends on how many garlic cloves are used, and that is a matter of personal taste. Today's version is almost indistinguishable from the *aïoli* of Provençal France, but originally the Spanish sauce consisted simply of crushed garlic with olive oil beaten in drop by drop to form an emulsion. Unfortunately, that technique is quite difficult to master, so egg yolks are almost always included in the modern version, resulting in a thicker, more stable sauce.

Allioli is quick and easy to make at home (see page 232), but few Spanish cooks bother because their supermarkets stock numerous brands. (Whenever you do make your own, however, store it in the refrigerator in a covered container and use within 3 days.)

The Fried Potatoes recipe (see page 247) combines the Spaniards' passion for fried foods with their love of potatoes, which appear in various guises in the different regions. These potatoes are a typically Spanish accompaniment to any grilled meat, seafood or poultry dishes.

Rice, like vegetables, is rarely served as a side-dish accompaniment in Spain, but several recipes are included in this chapter to help with meal planning in other countries. Artichoke Hearts and Peas (see page 248) is almost a meal in itself. Sherry Rice (see page 243) is a sophisticated side dish that complements a roast joint of veal or pork, as well as

When temperatures are soaring, try icy-cold Lemon Water. Its slightly bitter flavour is more refreshing than sweet lemonade.

Veal with Pickled Vegetables (see page 139). The recipe for Saffron Rice with Green Vegetables (see page 244) is ideal for turning even the simplest grilled lamb chop into a meal.

When temperatures are soaring, try icy cold Lemon Water (see page 252). Its slightly bitter flavour is more refreshing than sweet lemonade. And the classic Sangria (see page 253), the country's favourite choice for summer quaffing, is the perfect way to enjoy the full red wines of Spain and its sun-ripened fruits, combined in a long cool glass.

232

garlic mayonnaise
allioli

One of the classic sauces of Catalan cuisine. This is often served with fried seafood and tapas as a dip, but it is also excellent with simply cooked young vegetables in the spring. (Cook young, tender asparagus, baby carrots and new potatoes in individual saucepans of lightly salted boiling water until just tender-crisp. Drain and refresh with iced water to stop overcooking, then pat dry. Arrange a selection on each plate and season with salt and pepper, then add a dollop of Allioli on the side.)

Originally this Spanish sauce was distinctly different from French aïoli because it didn't include egg yolks. The authentic sauce, however, was difficult to make, so today there really isn't any difference between the two versions of garlic mayonnaise.

MAKES ABOUT 350 ML/12 FL OZ

3–4 large garlic cloves, or to taste
sea salt
2 large egg yolks
1 tsp lemon juice
300 ml/¹⁄₂ pint extra virgin olive oil
salt and pepper

1 Mash the garlic cloves to a paste with a pinch of sea salt. Put the paste in a food processor, add the egg yolks and lemon juice and process.

2 With the motor still running, slowly dribble in the olive oil through the feed tube until an emulsion forms and the sauce thickens. Taste and adjust the seasoning. Cover and chill for up to 3 days.

variation - Garlic Saffron Sauce
Soak a large pinch of saffron in 2 tablespoons of hot water for at least 10 minutes. Follow the recipe, and add the saffron water after the sauce thickens in step 2.

This Catalan tomato sauce is traditionally served with fish and shellfish, but it is also ideal for adding an instant Spanish flavour to simply cooked chicken, pork or lamb. Authentic recipes are made with dried romesco chillies, which have a sweet and hot flavour. Unfortunately, they are difficult to obtain outside the region, so this recipe uses a dried ñora chilli, which is another sweet variety, with dried hot chillies for the heat.

romesco sauce 233
romesco

MAKES ABOUT 300 ML/¹/₂ PINT

4 large, ripe tomatoes

16 blanched almonds (see page 50)

3 large garlic cloves, unpeeled and left whole

1 dried sweet chilli, such as ñora, soaked for
   20 minutes and patted dry

4 dried red chillies, soaked for 20 minutes and
   patted dry

pinch of sugar

150 ml/¹/₄ pint extra virgin olive oil

about 2 tbsp red wine vinegar

salt and pepper

1 Place the tomatoes, almonds and garlic on a baking sheet and roast in a preheated oven, 180°C/350°F/Gas Mark 4, for 20 minutes, but check the almonds after about 7 minutes, because they can burn quickly; remove as soon as they are golden and giving off an aroma.

2 Peel the roasted garlic and tomatoes. Put the almonds, garlic, sweet chilli and dried red chillies in a food processor and process until finely chopped. Add the tomatoes and sugar and process again.

3 With the motor running, slowly add the olive oil through the feed tube. Add 1¹/₂ tablespoons of the vinegar and quickly process. Taste and add extra vinegar, if desired, and salt and pepper to taste.

4 Leave to stand for at least 2 hours, then serve at room temperature. Alternatively, cover and chill for up to 3 days, then bring to room temperature before serving. Stir in any oil that separates before serving.

Like ratatouille from neighbouring France, this stew is best in the height of summer when vegetable gardens are at their most bountiful. Spaniards often serve this chilled, when it makes a flavoursome salad or tapas spooned onto thick bread slices. Served hot, it makes an ideal accompaniment to grilled chicken breasts or steaks.

This version cooks vegetables individually so the flavours remain distinctive.

SERVES 4–6

about 125 ml/4 fl oz olive oil

2 large onions, sliced thinly

4 large garlic cloves, crushed

300 g/10 oz aubergine, cut into 1-cm/^{1}/$_2$-inch cubes

300 g/10 oz yellow or green courgettes, cut into
    1-cm/^{1}/$_2$-inch cubes

1 large red pepper, cored, deseeded and chopped

1 large yellow pepper, cored, deseeded and chopped

1 large green pepper, cored, deseeded and chopped

2 sprigs fresh thyme

1 bay leaf

1 small sprig young rosemary

100 ml/3^1/$_2$ fl oz vegetable stock

salt and pepper

450 g/1 lb large, juicy tomatoes, peeled (see page 63),
    deseeded and chopped

mixed vegetable stew
pisto

1 Heat about 2 tablespoons of the oil in a large, flameproof casserole over a medium heat. Add the onions and fry, stirring occasionally, for about 5 minutes until they start to soften, but not brown. Add the garlic and stir around. Reduce the heat to very low.

2 Meanwhile, heat a frying pan over a high heat until you can feel the heat rising. Add 1 tablespoon of the oil and the aubergine cubes to make a single layer. Fry, stirring, until they are slightly brown on all sides. Add to the casserole with the onions.

3 Add another tablespoon of oil to the frying pan. Add the courgettes and fry, stirring, until lightly browned all over. Add the courgettes to the casserole. Fry the peppers the same way, then add to the casserole.

4 Stir the thyme, bay leaf, rosemary, stock and salt and pepper to taste into the casserole and bring to the boil. Reduce the heat to very low again, cover and simmer, stirring occasionally, for about 20 minutes until the vegetables are very tender and blended.

5 Remove the casserole from the heat and stir in the tomatoes. Cover and set aside for 10 minutes for the tomatoes to soften. The *pisto* is now ready to serve, but it is even better if it is left to cool completely and then served chilled the next day.

236

tomato and pepper sauce
salsa de tomates y pimientos

The amount of orange rind you add to this simple, all-purpose sauce really changes its character. Large strips of rind, for example, 'lift' the flavours in winter when fresh tomatoes are insipid.

MAKES ABOUT 700 ML/1¹/₄ PINTS

4 tbsp olive oil

10 large garlic cloves

140 g/5 oz shallots, chopped

4 large red peppers, cored, deseeded and chopped

1 kg/2 lb 4 oz good-flavoured ripe, fresh tomatoes, chopped, or 1.2 kg/2lb 12 oz good-quality canned chopped tomatoes

2 thin strips freshly pared orange rind

pinch hot red pepper flakes (optional), to taste

salt and pepper

1 Heat the olive oil in a large, flameproof casserole over a medium heat. Add the garlic, shallots and peppers and fry for about 10 minutes, stirring occasionally, until the peppers are soft, but not brown.

2 Add the tomatoes, including the juices if using canned ones, orange rind, hot pepper flakes, if using, and salt and pepper to taste and bring to the boil. Reduce the heat to as low as possible and simmer, uncovered, for 45 minutes, or until the liquid evaporates and the sauce thickens.

3 Purée the sauce through a mouli. Alternatively, purée in a food processor, then use a wooden spoon to press through a fine sieve. Taste and adjust the seasoning if necessary. Use at once, or cover and chill for up to 3 days.

Monteagudo in the province of Murcia, where irrigated soils yield vast quantities of rice, vegetables and fruit for the Spanish table

spinach with chickpeas 239
espinacas con garbanzos

Chickpeas have featured in Andalusian recipes for centuries, and Spanish conquistadors took this rich, nutty pulse with them on their long voyages of discovery to the New World. The use of cumin, cayenne and turmeric in this recipe reflects the North African and Moorish influences on Spanish cuisine. Serve this with any roast or grilled meat, or on its own as a vegetarian dish.

SERVES 4–6

2 tbsp olive oil

1 large garlic clove, cut in half

1 medium onion, chopped finely

^{1}/$_2$ tsp cumin

pinch cayenne pepper

pinch turmeric

800 g/1^3/$_4$ lb canned chickpeas, drained and rinsed

500 g/18 oz baby spinach leaves, rinsed and shaken dry

2 pimientos del piquillo (see page 67), drained and sliced

salt and pepper

1 Heat the oil in a large, lidded frying pan over a medium-high heat. Add the garlic and fry for 2 minutes, or until golden, but not brown. Remove with a slotted spoon and discard.

2 Add the onion and cumin, cayenne and turmeric and fry, stirring, about 5 minutes until soft. Add the chickpeas and stir around until they are lightly coloured with the turmeric and cayenne.

3 Stir in the spinach with just the water clinging to its leaves. Cover and cook for 4–5 minutes until wilted. Uncover, stir in the *pimientos del piquillo* and continue cooking, stirring gently, until all the liquid evaporates. Season to taste and serve.

Overleaf *An outdoor market offers not only a wide selection of fresh fruit and vegetables, but also the perfect opportunity to study local culture and customs*

sherry rice

arroz al jerez

An excellent dish to accompany roast veal, pork or chicken.

SERVES 4–6

2 tbsp olive oil

1 large onion, chopped finely

1 large garlic clove, crushed

400 g/14 oz Spanish short-grain rice

225 ml/8 fl oz amontillado sherry

1 litre/1³/4 pints fresh chicken stock, hot*

pinch of cayenne pepper

salt and pepper

1 Heat the oil in a shallow, heavy-based flameproof casserole. Add the onion and fry for about 3 minutes, then add the garlic and fry for a further 2 minutes, or until the onion is soft, but not brown.

2 Rinse the rice until the water runs clear. Drain, then add to the casserole and stir until it is coated in the oil. Add all but 2 tablespoons of the sherry and let it bubble. Pour in the stock with the cayenne and salt and pepper to taste and bring to the boil. Reduce the heat and leave to simmer for 20 minutes, uncovered and without stirring, until most of the stock is absorbed and small holes appear on the surface.

3 Turn off the heat under the rice, sprinkle with the remaining sherry, cover and leave for 10 minutes until all the liquid is absorbed.

variation – Saffron Sherry Rice

Bring the stock to the boil in a small saucepan, add a pinch of saffron threads, and set aside for at least 10 minutes to infuse. Follow the recipe above and use the saffron-flavoured stock in step 2.

*cook's tip

It is important not to use stock made from a cube, which tends to be salty and which would mask the delicate flavour of this dish.

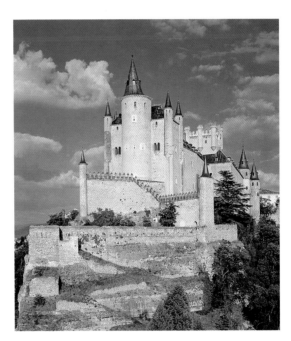

Castles in the air tell of Spain's glorious past

244

saffron rice with green vegetables
arroz azafranado con verduras

SERVES 4–6

large pinch saffron threads

1.2 litres/2 pints vegetable stock, hot

2 tbsp extra virgin olive oil

1 large onion, chopped finely

1 large garlic clove, crushed

400 g/14 oz short-grain Spanish rice

100 g/3^1/$_2$ oz French or other thin green beans, chopped

salt and pepper

100 g/3^1/$_2$ oz frozen peas

flat-leaved parsley, to garnish

1 Put the saffron threads in a heatproof bowl and add the hot vegetable stock; set aside to infuse.

2 Meanwhile, heat the oil in a shallow, heavy-based flameproof casserole over a medium-high heat. Add the onion and fry for about 3 minutes, then add the garlic and fry for a further 2 minutes, or until the onion is soft, but not brown.

3 Rinse the rice until the water runs clear. Drain, then add with the beans and stir until they are coated with oil. Pour in the stock with salt and pepper to taste and bring to the boil. Reduce the heat and leave to simmer for 12 minutes, uncovered, and without stirring.

4 Gently stir in the peas and continue simmering for 8 minutes until the liquid has been absorbed and the beans and peas are tender. Taste and adjust the seasoning. Garnish with the parsley and serve.

The sights of Madrid are as exciting and colourful by night as by day

fried potatoes
fritas

A popular Spanish way to prepare potatoes, one which is often served with meat or poultry, or as Feisty Potatoes (see page 86).

SERVES 6

1 kg/2 lb 4 oz potatoes, unpeeled

olive oil

sea salt

1 Scrub the potatoes, pat them dry and cut into chunky pieces.

2 Put 1 cm/$\frac{1}{2}$ inch olive oil and 1 potato piece in 1 of 2 large, heavy-based frying pans over a medium-high heat and heat until the potato begins to sizzle. Add the remaining potatoes, without crowding the pans, and fry for about 15 minutes until golden brown all over and tender. Work in batches, if necessary, keeping the cooked potatoes warm while you fry the remainder.

3 Use a slotted spoon to transfer the potatoes to a plate covered with crumpled kitchen paper. Blot off any excess oil and sprinkle with sea salt. Serve at once.

variation - Fried Garlic Potatoes
Thinly slice 6 large garlic cloves. Add to the frying pan with the potatoes, but only fry until they turn brown. Remove with a slotted spoon: if they burn, the oil will taste burnt. Alternatively, fry the potatoes in garlic-flavoured olive oil.

A rampant lion assumes pride of place among the monuments in Madrid

248

artichoke hearts and peas
alcachofas y guisantes

An ideal accompaniment to roast poultry, but delicious enough to become a light lunch in itself.

SERVES 4–6

4 tbsp extra virgin olive oil

2 onions, sliced finely

1 large garlic clove, crushed

280 g/10 oz artichoke hearts preserved in oil, drained and halved

200 g/7 oz frozen or fresh shelled peas

2 red peppers, grilled, deseeded (see page 74) and sliced

2 thin slices serrano ham, chopped (optional), or prosciutto

6 tbsp finely chopped fresh parsley

juice $1/2$ lemon

salt and pepper

1 Heat the oil in a flameproof casserole over a medium-high heat. Add the onions and fry, stirring, for 3 minutes, then add the garlic and fry for a further 2 minutes until the onions are soft, but not brown.

2 Add the halved artichoke hearts and fresh peas, if using, along with just enough water to cover. Bring to the boil, then reduce the heat and simmer for 5 minutes, uncovered, or until the peas are cooked through and all the water has evaporated.

3 Stir in the peppers, ham and frozen peas, if using. Continue simmering just long enough to warm through. Stir in the parsley and lemon juice to taste. Add salt and pepper, remembering that the ham is salty. Serve at once, or leave to cool to room temperature.

Beautifully designed fountains are among the many splendours of Madrid

hot chocolate 251
chocolate

1 Melt the chocolate in the milk in a heavy-based saucepan over a medium heat, stirring constantly. Add the sugar and continue stirring until it dissolves.

2 Put the cornflour in a small bowl and make a well in the centre. Add about 2 tablespoons of the hot liquid and gradually stir the cornflour into the liquid until a thick, smooth paste forms. Stir in another 2 tablespoons of hot liquid.

3 Stir all the cornflour mixture into the saucepan and bring to a simmer, stirring. Bring to the boil and continue stirring until the chocolate thickens. Pour into coffee cups and serve.

Spaniards love their hot chocolate so thick that it has a coating consistency and you almost need to eat it with a spoon – ideal for dipping in churros, Fried Pastries *(see page 221), a great breakfast treat. A small amount of this drink goes a long way because it is so rich.*

SERVES 4–6

100 g/3^1/$_2$ oz plain chocolate, with at least 70% cocoa, broken up

600 ml/1 pint milk

115 g/4 oz caster sugar

3^1/$_2$ tbsp cornflour

1 tsp vanilla essence

pinch salt

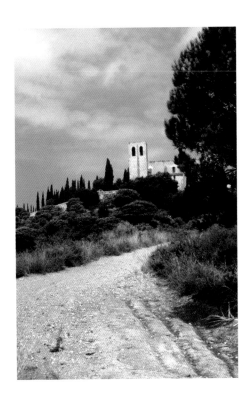

The sight of a bell tower announces a settlement to the traveller on this steep track

lemon water
agua limón

MAKES 4–6 GLASSES

8 large lemons

200 g/7 oz caster sugar, plus extra to taste

700 ml/1 1/4 pints boiling water

1 Finely grate the rind and squeeze the juice of 7 of the lemons into a large heatproof bowl; remove all the seeds. Finely slice the remaining lemon and reserve 4–6 slices to use for serving; stir the remainder into the juice.

2 Stir the caster sugar into the bowl. Add the boiling water and leave to cool to room temperature. Chill until required.

3 To serve, strain into a serving jug and dilute with cold water to taste. Stir in extra sugar, if desired. Serve in chilled glasses, garnishing each one with a slice of lemon.

sangria

sangría

MAKES 12–15 GLASSES

100 ml/3¹/₂ fl oz Spanish brandy

4 large lemons, sliced and quartered

4 large oranges, sliced and quartered

2 limes, sliced and quartered

2 peaches, stoned and sliced (optional)

2 x 75-cl bottles full-flavoured Spanish red wine, chilled

200 g/7 oz caster sugar, plus extra to taste

ice cubes, to serve

1 Put the brandy and half the citrus fruit and peach slices, if using, in a bowl and use a wooden spoon to crush the fruit into the brandy. Cover and chill for at least 2 hours. Cover the remaining fruit slices and chill until required.

2 Pour the brandy and fruit into a large serving jug, add the wine and the sugar, stirring until dissolved. Taste and add extra sugar, if desired. Place a mixture of the reserved fruit slices in glasses and pour over the Sangria, including some of the brandy-soaked fruit.

index

index